GUIDE TO THE QUEHANNA TRAIL

SECOND EDITION

BEN CRAMER

CATAMOUNT
PRESS

an imprint of Sunbury Press, Inc.
Mechanicsburg, PA USA

an imprint of Sunbury Press, Inc.
Mechanicsburg, PA USA

FIRST CATAMOUNT PRESS EDITION: May 2026

Set in Adobe Garamond | Interior design by Crystal Devine | Cover by Lawrence Knorr | Edited by Debra Reynolds. All photos by David "Cyril" Quatrone.

Publisher's Cataloging-in-Publication Data
Names: Cramer, Ben, author.
Title: Guide to the Quehanna Trail / Ben Cramer.
Description: First trade paperback edition. | Mechanicsburg, PA : Catamount Press, 2026.
Summary: A point-by-point guide to the Quehanna Trail, a 73-mile loop trail that travels through Moshannon and Elk State Forests in Clearfield, Cameron, and Elk Counties, Pennsylvania. The guide also includes five affiliated trails and further descriptions of the surrounding landscape.
Identifiers: ISBN : 979-8-88819-450-8 (softcover).
Subjects: SPORTS & RECREATION / Hiking | TRAVEL / Northeast / Middle Atlantic (NJ, NJ, PA) | NATURE / Regional.

Designed in the USA
0 1 1 2 3 5 8 13 21 34 55

For the Love of Books!

Cover: The author (somewhere in the center) does an early morning inspection of the Quehanna Trail in one of its many meadows, near Piper.

TABLE OF CONTENTS

AUTHOR'S NOTE

This trail guide accurately reflects measurements and observations that were made along the Quehanna Trail and its affiliated trails during inspections by the author in spring and summer 2025. Original measurements taken for the previous edition of this guidebook in 2015 have been rechecked for accuracy and all relocated trail segments have been newly measured in full.

All efforts have been made to ensure accuracy in descriptions of the features and logistics of the trail, and the distances involved. However, conditions in the natural world are constantly changing. Fallen trees, flash floods, forestry practices, human developments, and myriad other phenomena often necessitate the rerouting of hiking trails and can damage infrastructure such as footbridges. Changes in the route or condition of the trail may be completed by the Pennsylvania Department of Conservation and Natural Resources, Keystone Trails Association, or other volunteers after this guide is published.

All persons using this guide do so at their own risk, and this guide should not be used without adequate maps and other common-sense precautions, which should be practiced by all outdoorspersons. The author, publisher, and all trail workers/volunteers disclaim any and all liability for trail conditions, hazards, incidents encountered by hikers, and inaccuracies in this guide that may be the result of future developments. Also, the reader should follow this guide's recommendations for water sources and camping locations at his/her own risk. Please contact the author about any changes encountered along the trails that should be included in future editions of this guide.

ACKNOWLEDGMENTS

The joy of hiking in Pennsylvania would not be possible without the contributions of volunteer trail builders, maintainers, and observers. Hikers and backpackers may not even notice the valuable work of these volunteers, but they would surely notice if all that hard work was no longer being performed. Thanks to all the trail club volunteers and state forest employees in Pennsylvania who make our trails so enjoyable.

This new edition of my *Guide to the Quehanna Trail* would not have been possible without the assistance of David "Cyril" Quatrone, who in 2025 accompanied me on my new inspections of most of the trails described in this book, adding his name to the list of people who have completed the Quehanna Trail in the process. Quatrone also took all the photographs in this book.

Special thanks to Bob Merrill and Al Germann of Keystone Trails Association for their help in finding information on plans by forestry officials to repair and upgrade parts of the Quehanna Trial that were in progress at the time of writing. Thanks also to Marge Guinard, Tom Guinard, and Janet Wolfe for their surprise hospitality when I encountered them at a remote campsite during one of my measuring projects.

I would also like to thank several people who helped with the first edition of this guidebook in 2015, namely Terri Davis and Terrie Young for transportation assistance, and volunteer trail maintainer Terry Detsch for crucial information on the Quehanna Trail's perennial challenges. Thanks also to DCNR employees Zac Miller, Doug Mohney, and Wally Finn for their invaluable assistance when showing me around the Corporation Dam area and explaining its natural and manmade history. Special thanks to Ralph Seeley for his longtime leadership in maintaining the Quehanna Trail and many nearby trails, and his wealth of historical and ecological knowledge.

And finally, many thanks to Brook Lenker of Keystone Trails Association for providing a connection with Sunbury Press, where Lawrence Knorr and everyone on his staff have been instrumental in getting this book into your hands.

Ben Cramer, December 2025

HIKING THE QUEHANNA TRAIL NETWORK

The Quehanna Trail at Saunders Road.

INTRODUCTION

The Quehanna Trail (QT) is a 73.73 mile long, oval-shaped loop trail in Moshannon and Elk State Forests in Central Pennsylvania. The trail passes through portions of Clearfield, Cameron, and Elk Counties. About 34 miles of the QT are within Quehanna Wild Area, the largest such designated area in Pennsylvania. The main road in the area is the paved Quehanna Highway, which leads northwest-southeast from PA 555 at Medix Run to PA 879 near Karthaus.

The QT was built in 1976–1977 as a state forestry project to improve recreational opportunities while providing work for at-risk youths and the underemployed (a method based on that of the famous Civilian Conservation Corps of the New Deal era). The trail was already deteriorating due to underuse by the 1980s, and widespread use of the QT and its affiliated trails did not really take off until the 1990s, when it was discovered by backpacking magazines and promoted in books like *50 Hikes in Central Pennsylvania* by the late Tom Thwaites.

The QT has three cross-connector trails that can be used to form shorter loop hikes or hiked in their own right: the Cut Off Trail (1.68 miles), the West Cross Connector Trail (6.27 miles) and the East Cross Connector Trail (9.35 miles). A spur known as the Old Sinnemahoning Trail (6.77 miles) can be used to reach the villages of Wyside and Sinnemahoning to the northeast. Another spur called the Bear Run Trail (5.27 miles) follows a former route of the QT in the northwestern portion of the network, and can be used to as a creative bypass of some of the main trail or simply enjoyed in its own right. All these trails are described in this guide.

The area traversed by these trails is among the most remote in Pennsylvania. Along Quehanna Highway, there are no permanent residents for more than 20 miles between Medix Run and Karthaus. The nearest sizable towns with full services are Clearfield, which is about 17 miles south of the QT trailhead at Parker Dam State Park via PA 153 or about 26 miles southwest of the southern portions of the QT via PA 879; and St. Marys, which is about 20 miles north of the QT trail network via PA 555 and PA 255. Some smaller villages nearby that offer a few convenient stores and local restaurants include Karthaus on PA 879, Benezette on PA 555, and Penfield on PA 153. You may also hear of a small town named Piper near the trail; this unique locality has an interesting history that will be described later in this book, but no conventional services for hikers.

The Quehanna Trail and its cross connectors sit on top of a high and windy Central Pennsylvania plateau between Sinnemahoning Creek to the north and the West Branch Susquehanna River to the south. The southern portions of the Quehanna Trail loop are generally flat or gently rolling and stay at a high elevation (usually above 1900 feet), with the exceptions of some minor dips into hollows and one significant plunge into the gorge formed by Mosquito Creek. The northern portions of the QT loop are more rugged, with frequent and tough climbs out of deeper hollows like those for Wykoff Run, Red Run, Sliver Mill Run, and Medix Run, separated by brief rambles on top of the flat plateau.

The southern portions of the QT loop traverse a mostly oak/laurel ecosystem engendered by the high elevations, with evergreens and rhododendrons mostly confined to hollows along streams. The hiker will notice the forest changing as he/she proceeds to the northern portions of the QT loop, with more hardwoods and evergreens coming into view. This area is known for particularly enormous rhododendron bushes in the hollows, especially on north-facing slopes.

The defining ecological features of the Quehanna Trail network are the large open meadows in the high plateau areas, of a type rarely seen elsewhere in Pennsylvania. The meadows are typically populated by ferns, huckleberry and similar low-lying shrubs, and short grasses. In recent years, many of these meadows have been managed to provide forage for deer and elk.

Some of these meadows are natural and are probably the result of poor drainage of rainwater and snowmelt in the flat areas on top of the plateau. The resulting soggy soil prevents the growth of trees. Other such meadows are not so natural, having been formed when logging, forest fires, beaver dams, and even tornadoes caused the disappearance of forested areas that failed to regenerate. In fact, the after-effects of the

One of the largest meadows in the Quehanna Trail network; this one is traversed by the East Cross Connector Trail.

infamous tornadoes of May 31, 1985, which ravaged large parts of Central and Northwestern Pennsylvania and are still talked about 40 years later, can be seen in several places in the Quehanna Trail network.

Note that the veteran trail builder and local historian Ralph Seeley has written extensively on the development of the QT and other nearby trails, as well as the history of the surrounding region going back to pioneer days. To avoid repetition, the author of the present trail guide wishes to direct interested persons to the source, to learn from the acknowledged expert in the field. Seeley's book *Greate Buffaloe Swamp* is a fascinating history of the region with descriptions of many of its hiking trails. There is also a condensed version called *Foot Trails of the Moshannon and Southern Elk State Forests* (4th edition, 2014). The first edition of this guide to the QT also benefited greatly from the author's personal communications with Seeley, and his wisdom continues to influence this new edition as well.

Whereas this guide contains a greater amount of detail for the hiker on the trails in the Quehanna network, Seeley's *Foot Trails of the Moshannon and Southern Elk State Forests* has been consulted for more historical and ecological information. Wherever relevant, this guide features page numbers next to the citation "[Seeley]" for readers who wish to find more information on some of the manmade and natural features encountered along the QT and its affiliated trails.

DAY HIKES AND BACKPACKING TRIPS

Due to its great length and far-flung road crossings, the Quehanna Trail is surely a backpacker's trail and arranging shorter day hikes is a challenge. However, beginners and day hikers should not be dissuaded from sampling the wonders of the trail.

The Quehanna plateau region, and especially Quehanna Wild Area, has well over 150 total miles of trails, which have been designated in various configurations for hiking, skiing, and horseback riding. For brevity, and also because of its focus on hiking, this particular book only describes the main trails that are used most often by hikers year-round:

Quehanna Trail, Cut Off Trail, West Cross Connector Trail, East Cross Connector Trail, Old Sinnemahoning Trail, and Bear Run Trail.

There are many other trails in the area, most of them relatively short paths designed for day hikers (these are usually yellow-blazed). In recent years, personnel at Moshannon and Elk State Forests have been transforming forgotten dirt roads and pipeline swaths for equestrians and mountain bikers, and sometimes for off-road vehicle enthusiasts (these are usually red-blazed.)

These additional trails are easily visible on the respective state forest maps and DCNR (Pennsylvania Department of Conservation and Natural Resources) maps. DCNR personnel and club volunteers are making great efforts to maintain and promote all these trails in the Quehanna region, as part of a "multi-use" philosophy. Because hiking is the outdoor sport with the least environmental impact (at least in terms of basic walking), hikers can actually use trails of any designation. On the contrary, horseback riders and mountain bikers are not allowed on trails that have been designated as hiking-only. There are also some trails in the area that are designated for cross-country skiing in the winter, which may sport blue blazes.

Hikers who are good at reading maps and estimating distances could consider using many of these area trails to form loops or shortcuts to parking spots while exploring the Quehanna Trail network. The aforementioned book *Foot Trails of the Moshannon and Southern Elk State Forests* by Ralph Seeley includes descriptions of many of the ski trails in Quehanna Wild Area.

Experienced backpackers could conceivably complete the entire Quehanna Trail in five or six days. Beginning backpackers, or those wishing for a relaxed pace, should prepare for at least seven days. There are many possibilities for loop hikes of various lengths on the cross-connector trails and other nearby paths (see the "Logistics of the Quehanna Trail Network" chapter below for details.)

In addition to short loop hikes where they can be arranged, the author of this book strongly recommends day hikes of the out-and-back variety. Start at one of the more accessible parking spots, follow the trail for a certain distance, then simply turn around and return to your car. Not only can you tell your friends that you have completed that section of the trail twice, but this is a useful technique for piecing together a series of day hikes into a complete transit of a long-distance trail. Besides, hikers are often surprised by how much scenery they can miss by following a trail in only one direction. Just note that the trail descriptions in this book are one-way so if you are going in the opposite direction, left turns become right turns, uphill becomes downhill, and the like.

CAMPING

Most of the Quehanna Trail and its affiliated connector trails are on State Forest land (including Quehanna Wild Area). Therefore, primitive camping and backpacking are permitted along the trails, except for some short segments that cross state game lands and Parker Dam State Park that are noted specifically in this guide.

Most of the trails described in this guide abound in pleasant locations for primitive backpacking. Many are near water sources, and in the case of the main Quehanna Trail loop they are fairly evenly distributed, which will make the planning of multi-night backpacking trips more convenient. Also, overnighters and beginners could practice primitive camping techniques by parking at a convenient spot and hiking in a short distance on the trail.

Primitive camping spots that backpackers would consider "favorable"—a flat spot with a nearby stream and shady trees overhead—are quite common in the network of trails described in this guide, except for the Old Sinnemahoning Trail on which they are completely nonexistent. Primitive backpacking is still possible wherever you may find yourself, but some locations will offer a rougher experience.

In Pennsylvania State Forest terminology, backcountry camping comes in two flavors: "car camping" (where you can park directly at a campsite) and "primitive camping" (on foot with a backpack). The latter is permitted anywhere in State Forest lands, with some restrictions as listed below.

In Moshannon and Elk State Forests, statewide camping rules apply. The Pennsylvania Department of Conservation and Natural Resources (DCNR) maintains rules and regulations for primitive camping on State

Forest lands. The Commonwealth utilizes camping permits, which are mostly used for recordkeeping and safety purposes, and are free of charge at the time of this writing. Also at the time of writing, primitive back-packers are not required to apply for a camping permit except if any of the following conditions apply:

- An emergency point of contact is desired.
- You plan to stay at the same site for more than one night.
- A campfire is planned during the spring or fall fire seasons.
- You are "group camping" (more than 10 people.)

This process is designed to control the damage that could result from large numbers of campers in sensitive areas. Note that camping permits are not issued to persons under 18. To apply for a camping permit, visit the DCNR website at www.dcnr.pa.gov. The site will direct you to navigate to the page for the applicable state forest district office where you will then find the necessary contact information and instructions.

Important Primitive Camping Rules: DCNR maintains many rules for primitive camping in the state forests. Some of these will seem like common sense to experienced outdoorspersons, but others are unique to Pennsylvania conditions. For the most up-to-date rules, see the official state document "Motorized and Primitive Camping Guidelines and Eth-ics" which can also be found at the DCNR website.

Backpackers in Pennsylvania should observe the following important rules, among others:

- Carry out all trash. Repeat: ALL trash.
- Choose a spot that does not require the clearing of vegetation.
- Stay at least 100 feet away from any flowing stream or open water source.
- Do not wash clothes, dishes, or campsite equipment directly in a stream or spring. Collect water in a container and do your washing away from the source, then dispose of the wastewater at least 200 feet from the source.
- Whenever possible, camp at least 25 feet from the trail, and preferably out of sight of the trail.

- Dispose of human waste by burying it in a hole at least 6 inches deep. Bring a camp trowel or small shovel for this purpose. Disposal sites should be at least 200 feet from water sources.
- Do not build a campfire during the dry seasons of spring and fall, or during other periods of abnormally high fire danger. At other times, small campfires are permitted. At previously unused campsites, construct a fire ring with nearby rocks to prevent the flames from spreading, and scatter the ring before leaving the site.
- Do not chop down live trees for firewood. Only use downed and dead wood near your campsite. Power saws are not permitted except with prior permission from the relevant state forest office.

Also, though it is not a State Forest rule, beware of camping in or near copses of giant rhododendron and mountain laurel. These plants are flammable and may also provide cover for disagreeable animals.

Camping Locations Mentioned in This Guide: The author has made an effort to point out potential primitive camping spots along the trails, with selections being made for variety and the potential for pleasant backpacking experiences. However, not all of these sites may completely comply with the above rules. Some areas within larger "sites" listed in this guide may not be 100 feet from a water source or 25 feet from the trail. The hiker will also notice many existing campsites created by previous backpackers, which may not comply with either of those strictures. The mention of such sites in this guide should not be considered an endorsement of the possibly illegal activities of previous backpackers.

Many of the possible campsites mentioned in this guide are near streams and springs, and to follow the state forest rules you would have to find a spot along the edge of such an area that is sufficiently removed from the water. All backpackers are strongly advised to follow the DCNR's primitive camping rules, which will ensure that future backpackers will not be deprived of the opportunity. Those using this guide will camp at the described spots at their own risk.

WATER

Mix Run as seen from a footbridge on the
Quehanna Trail.

In this age of acid rain and bacterial pathogens, all water sources encountered in the wild should be viewed with suspicion. Most of the trails in the Quehanna region encounter plentiful streams and springs, and the natural water supply in this highland area is fairly clean compared to that in nearby valley areas, notwithstanding a few exceptions described in this guide. It must be noted that some spots within Quehanna Wild Area have experienced radioactive contamination in the past, though state officials have apparently concluded that this has not affected the general water supply. (See "Appendix B: Piper and Quehanna Wild Area" later in this book.)

Giardia, a waterborne bacterium that causes the gastro-intestinal illness giardiasis, has been found in mountain streams throughout Pennsylvania. While experienced outdoorspersons might be comfortable drinking wild water, no hiking guide (including this one) will recommend doing so, and such actions will be taken at your own risk.

Water found along the trail should be treated with iodine capsules or submicron filters, which can be found at sports stores and outfitters. This is the recommended strategy for backpackers. The old-school method of purifying water by boiling it at a campfire is a tedious chore that is usually not worth the effort, even when boiling is actually achieved via a small wood fire. Day hikers should have little difficulty merely packing up the water they will need at home before embarking on their day trips.

Water Sources Listed in This Guide: As of 2025, the present author has completed all the trails described in this guide multiple times during various seasons of the year, and has made an effort in this guide to describe the quality and seasonality of the water sources encountered along the trails. However, the user of this guide will consume any water found along the trail at his/her own risk. As a general rule, water found in muddy spots, seep springs, and backwaters along the sides of flowing streams should be avoided. Also, water from larger creeks should be avoided because wide waterways, by definition, have collected water from many tributaries and low-lying areas, increasing the chances of pollution. Also avoid taking water from streams that feature beaver dams, which alter natural filtration patterns.

This guide describes the suspected water quality (in the experienced hiker's estimation) of the many springs and small streams encountered along the trails discussed. These readings were not determined scientifically, should not be taken as any type of recommendation to drink the water, and should be considered as loose guidelines only. Water sources listed here as "poor" or "not suitable" should be avoided under all circumstances. Sources described as "questionable" could possibly be consumed by the desperate, or hikers with high-quality filters, though such actions should be unnecessary in this region because better sources are almost always available nearby. A fair number of water sources are described as "acceptable," "good," or "excellent" in this guide. Water from these sources can be consumed by any hiker with store-bought filtering equipment.

A final note on water sources described in this guide: If you visit the trails during an especially dry period, beware that the flow and quality of springs and streams as described in this guide may be reduced. In fact, some may not even be flowing by the time you reach them. Wherever possible, efforts have been made to determine the quality of water sources during various seasons.

WILDLIFE

An eastern timber rattlesnake spotted on the Quehanna Trail near Laurel Draft.

Moshannon and Elk State Forests feature the wildlife that is typical for forested areas of Central Pennsylvania. White-tailed deer are very prevalent in the region, as are smaller forest denizens such as chipmunks, squirrels, mice, groundhogs, and rabbits. Areas of forest that have been over-browsed by deer (notable by the preponderance of ferns) are somewhat common in the QT network. However, deer are almost always harmless and will typically flee from human contact.

Birdwatchers may be treated to sightings of golden eagles, bald eagles, wild turkeys, a variety of hawks, and even bluebirds, all of which have been spotted in the area by the author. Patience might be rewarded by sightings of the many common and not-so-common species of songbirds that are native to the area.

Rare sightings of fishers (larger relatives of weasels and ferrets) and bobcats have also been reported in the area. Meanwhile, the hiker may hear reports of mountain lions—reports that are on the increase in Central Pennsylvania. For the time being such reports should be treated with skepticism, though local nature lovers can hope that this kingly beast will reclaim its ancestral homeland.

Predators should not be a serious concern for hikers if one exercises common sense. There are black bears in the region, but they tend to flee from humans long before they are seen, thanks to their remarkable sense of smell. A hiker should consider it great luck to even see one. Bears should not be provoked and definitely should not be fed, which increases the chances of their behavior changing abruptly from docile to aggressive.

There is a chance of bears harassing untended campsites, though this should not be a serious concern for backpackers who take the necessary precautions. Porcupines and coyotes are also common in the area, and these scavengers have been known to disturb untended campsites. However, both of these animals are quite skittish and are highly unlikely to confront humans directly.

The only truly dangerous animal in this area is the eastern timber rattlesnake. This snake prefers open areas for sunning and rocky outcrops for building dens. This species is venomous, but its bites are typically not fatal to healthy humans, with only a medium-strength temporary illness resulting for most people. (However, some people are highly allergic to the venom, leading to a more serious illness, and are probably unaware of their allergy until it is too late. Also, extra vigilance should be exercised for one's smaller hiking companions, such as dogs and young children.)

If bitten by a rattlesnake along the trail, do not panic. Return to your car quickly but in a level-headed manner; and seek medical attention as soon as possible. Contrary to popular opinion, rattlesnakes rarely attack humans, but rather defend themselves when provoked. In a telling reflection of human nature, upwards of 80% of snakebite victims anywhere in the world are bitten on their hands and arms, after stupidly trying to pick up the snake. In the rare event that you encounter an eastern timber rattlesnake, retreat sensibly, leave it alone, and consider yourself lucky to have seen this unique creature in its natural habitat.

A different problem arises from insects. Mosquitoes and similar pests are ubiquitous in the region, as are ticks. Lyme Disease has been reported in the area, and encounters with ticks (only a few of which actually carry the disease) are on the rise. High-quality insect repellent is crucial on Pennsylvania hiking trails during all seasons except the deepest parts of Winter.

There is one additional critter that deserves an honorable mention here. Beavers are very common in the region and their resolute landscaping endeavors are often quite visible along some of the trails described in this book, especially the East Cross Connector Trail which has been rerouted several times due to the critters' activities.

Elk: This majestic animal is native to Pennsylvania and once roamed across the state. Due to unregulated hunting and habitat loss, elk were extinct throughout most of Pennsylvania by the 1850s, with a tiny population hanging on in the present Elk and Cameron Counties. Those last few holdouts were gone by about 1880. Efforts to reintroduce elk to Central Pennsylvania go back as far as 1912, when plans were hatched to import a small population (by train) from Yellowstone National Park.

Thanks to this and a few other deliveries, a small population of elk reestablished themselves in the plateau region of Central Pennsylvania but got themselves into trouble by wandering onto farms. The "solution" to this problem was hunting, with the first official elk season declared in 1923. History repeated itself, and by the 1950s the population of elk was again reduced to just a few dozen hanging on in Elk and Cameron Counties. Thanks to new research on managing elk behavior and various methods of alleviating the concerns of landowners, the elk population had recovered a bit by the 1990s. The state has since initiated new efforts to relocate individuals to specially designated areas, while introducing new fencing technologies and habitat management strategies to encourage the elk to stay near home.

At the time of this writing in 2025, Pennsylvania heavily advertises it elk herd as an ecotourist attraction and estimates the current population to be about 1,400 individuals. This is a significant increase over the last few decades, even with limited hunting, which is permitted through a lottery process in which just a few hunters are allowed to harvest an elk if they see one.

Hikers are most likely to see elk to the north of the QT network, on the aptly named Elk Trail as well as the Donut Hole Trail and Bucktail Path. I have seen elk on those trails multiple times. I have also seen elk hanging around the streets in Benezette (apparently not a big deal to the residents) and once saw a large herd simply browsing in someone's front yard in the village of Sinnemahoning on PA 120. I personally have not seen elk on the Quehanna Trail, though many other people have reported doing so, particularly above Mix Run and Wykoff Run in the northern portions of the loop. Elk have also been reported at Parker Dam State Park, lounging in the softball field.

While it is a great joy to see elk, exercise caution and common sense. Elk are social animals and typically travel in herds, except for young adult males who tend to hang together in groups of two or three. Avoid approaching an elk closely—an adult is as big as a horse but not nearly as dumb. An adult male's enormous antlers can do some serious damage in self-defense.

From my personal experience and that of several fellow hikers who have come across elk in the wild, there should be little trouble if you keep your distance. If elk are browsing, they may not notice you approaching at first. When they do notice you, they will probably stare at you until they figure out if you are a threat; if so, they will run in the other direction. If you are acting calmly, the elk will eventually get bored looking at you and amble away in a relaxed fashion.

I must also make note of the story of one colleague who came across two young adult male elk while hiking. One departed while the other stood still, allowing my colleague to look at him for an extended period. It turned out that the first elk had circled around behind the gentleman and he found himself surrounded. The story ended happily, because apparently these bulls just wanted to flush the guy out of their territory.

IMPORTANT: These stories are based on limited experience and should not be construed as a guarantee of elk behavior if you happen to come across any while hiking. Like bears and rattlesnakes, consider yourself luck to see the animal, then behave responsibly and sensibly. Also, there is no guarantee that you will see elk or any other animal during a particular hike, though you might get lucky, and multiple trips to the area will eventually be rewarded.

A Note on Hunting: The plentiful wildlife in this area attracts a thriving hunting industry, and hikers must exercise caution in the presence of hunters. The author of this guide and the associated trail maintainers and Commonwealth personnel disavow all responsibility for the danger in which hikers may place themselves when hunters are present. Avoid hiking in State Forest areas during the big game hunting seasons in the fall and early winter. If necessary, inquire with State Forest personnel beforehand to learn which areas of the forest attract the most hunters. The Pennsylvania Game Commission also manages hunting seasons for many types of small game throughout the rest of the year, though these seasons present little risk for the hiker. Nevertheless, anyone hiking in areas known to be frequented by hunters is strongly advised to wear at least one prominent piece of "safety orange" clothing for visibility.

LOGISTICS OF THE QUEHANNA TRAIL NETWORK

A red eft spotted on the Quehanna Trail near Trout Run.

Your present author has personally measured all of the trails described in this guide, first during a series of day hikes from late 2014 to early 2015 for the first edition of this book. All measurements were verified for accuracy again in mid-2025 for the second edition that you are holding in your hands. Here are the latest recorded lengths of these trails:

Quehanna Trail: 73.73 mi (118.73 km)
Cut Off Trail: 1.68 mi (2.71 km)
West Cross Connector Trail: 6.27 mi (10.10 km)
East Cross Connector Trail: 9.35 mi (15.06 km)
Old Sinnemahoning Trail: 6.77 mi (10.90 km)
Bear Run Trail: 5.27 mi (8.49 km)

For this new edition of the guide, I hiked the entire trail network again and found that the Cut Off Trail, East Cross Connector Trail, and Old Sinnemahoning Trail were unchanged. However, I made note of a whopping fourteen relocations along the main Quehanna Trail since my previous guide in 2015, most of which were built to bypass chronically soggy areas or environmentally sensitive spots. There was also a significant rerouting of the QT in its northwest quadrant along Medix Run, which abandoned more than five miles of the former route and appropriated the northernmost segment of the West Cross Connector Trail. (For more on this series of events, see "Appendix C: Medix Run and the Bear Run Trail.")

The abandoned QT route is now known as Bear Run Trail and the West Cross Connector Trail is more than three miles shorter than it was in 2015. Of the many relocations around the QT, some added a little distance to the trail, some subtracted a little, and the Medix Run reroute subtracted a lot. This resulted in a net loss of distance for the main Quehanna Trail, and its current length of 73.73 miles is about half a mile shorter than it was for the 2015 edition of this guide.

Over its lifetime since the 1970s, the main Quehanna Trail has been subjected to many relocations and volunteer measurements ranging from reliable to downright dubious. Before the first edition of this guide in 2015, to my knowledge the only precise on-the-ground measurement of the QT was by the late Tom Thwaites in the 1990s, for an early edition of his book *50 Hikes in Central Pennsylvania*. At that time, Thwaites measured the QT at approximately 73 miles. It had become a little longer by 2015 and has since become a little shorter.

Also, over the trail's history, various maps, books, recreational promotions, and other items have described the QT as anywhere from 69 to 76 miles. The lower and higher ends of that range are curious and were probably very loose estimates at best. The Pennsylvania Department of Conservation and Natural Resources (DCNR) has published periodic maps of the QT network that are available for free at State Forest/State Park offices and at many roadside kiosks. These maps have included distances for the trails, but I have found these to be significantly inaccurate and almost always lower than reality. Some older editions of this map included the ungratifying disclaimer "The trail mileage shown on this map was obtained by map measurements and may differ from actual walking distance because of slope." At the time of this writing, the most recent such map was published in 2019; that version includes several errors though it is very informative for planning purposes.

And finally, as a hiking trail guidebook author, I beseech you to treat online measurements of trails, contributed by hikers to user-generated sites like AllTrails, with the utmost suspicion. Unless the contributor tells you otherwise, assume that such measurements were made by smartphones or wearable fitness devices, the accuracy of which have never been demonstrated convincingly; while the online services have little or no oversight by those who could verify the measurements for accuracy. Consumer-grade mobile devices tend to over-measure a hike because of a technical problem called GPS drift, in which the software records you as still moving even when you are not moving during a break, due to the vagaries of satellite orbits and the rotation of the earth below. Such errors can be corrected with professional mapping software, as has been done for this book by your present author, but which is almost never done by semi-anonymous contributors to unreliable online services.

MEASUREMENT TECHNIQUE FOR THIS BOOK

Most of the trail measurements for the first edition of this guide were recorded via a measuring wheel, which hiking trail maintainers have accepted as the tool with the greatest accuracy. The wheel is pushed along the ground, and an odometer measures the distance by the foot or meter, leading to concise measurements that have been demonstrated as quite consistent among multiple people who have measured the same trail. I simultaneously carried a Garmin handheld GPS device to record the routes of the trails, point-by-point across the surface of the earth, but usually not to record distance unless absolutely needed.

While in the middle of that earlier project, my measuring wheel broke and due to time pressures, I collected some distance measurements with the GPS device. With sufficient practice in managing the resulting raw GPS data via professional mapping software, I became confident that the data was as accurate as the measurements made with the wheel.

The accuracy of on-the-ground distance measurements via GPS has not yet been fully acknowledged by trail maintainers and veteran hikers, though most have accepted the accuracy of GPS mapping. I am confident of the accuracy of the GPS distance measurements featured in this guide, so please accept the figures as "official" until the next volunteer comes along to measure all the trails again.

For all relocations detected during my 2025 inspection of the trails, I measured the new trail segments with a newer measuring wheel in a quest for the greatest possible accuracy. In the final pages of this book you will find small maps, plus a QR code and website address that can be used to access a more detailed online map. All of these were created with my carefully verified GPS data.

PLANNING FOR LONG-DISTANCE HIKES

You are encouraged to use the Quehanna Trail network for car shuttle hikes, out-and-back hikes, and short loops, in addition to extended backpacking trips. For the planning of hikes, this guide describes the main Quehanna Trail loop in a counterclockwise fashion, starting at the official trailhead in Parker Dam State Park. This is how the QT has been described traditionally. The Cut Off Trail and West Cross Connector Trail have been described in the northbound direction; the East Cross Connector and Old Sinnemahoning Trail have been described in the southbound direction. These are also the traditional methods of describing those trails, because it makes planning loop hikes easier. The newly designated Bear Run Trail is described in the westbound direction to match its previous existence as a segment of the QT.

In addition to a 5–7 day backpacking loop on the Quehanna Trail itself (see the last chapter), veteran hikers have long promoted the following easy-to-ambitious circuit hikes in the Quehanna Trail network.

- Cut Off Trail Loop: This highly recommended loop can be completed in a robust day hike of about 3–4 hours. Starting from the trailhead at Parker Dam State Park, follow the Quehanna Trail to mile 3.47, then turn north on the Cutoff Trail which is 1.68

miles long. Then turn west on the other end of the Quehanna Trail and follow it 2.29 miles back to the trailhead. The total distance of this loop is 7.44 miles.

- West Loop: This loop makes use of the western ends of the main Quehanna Trail and can be completed in a very long day hike, or more likely as a nice introductory 2-day backpacking trip. Starting from the trailhead at Parker Dam State Park, follow the Quehanna Trail to mile 4.95, then turn northeast on the West Cross Connector Trail which is 6.27 miles long. Then turn west on the other end of the Quehanna Trail and follow it 8.59 miles back to the trailhead. The total distance of this loop is 19.81 miles. Due to a shortage of viable campsites in the middle reaches of this loop, prepare for one long day and one short day of backpacking
- East Loop: This loop makes use of the eastern segments of the Quehanna Trail. The parking areas on Quehanna Highway near Piper or Wykoff Run Road are good places to start this 3–4 day backpacking loop. Use the East Cross Connector Trail, which is 9.35 miles long, and the main Quehanna Trail from the 20.24 mi to 51.70 mi points. This loop is 40.81 miles long.
- Middle Loop: This loop traverses the center of the network, using both the West Cross Connector Trail and East Cross Connector Trail, plus two intervening segments of the Quehanna Trail to the north and south. The parking lot on Quehanna Highway at Haystack Mountain (QT) or another lot on that same road near Beaver Run Wildlife Viewing Area (East Cross Connector) would be convenient for this 3–4 day backpacking loop. Use the main Quehanna Trail between its 51.70 mi and 65.14 mi points; all 6.27 miles of the West Cross Connector; the main QT from its 4.95 mi to 20.24 mi points; and all 9.35 miles of the East Cross Connector. This loop is 44.35 miles long.

The Quehanna Trail network is also within reach of another long-distance Pennsylvania backpacking trail, via the Old Sinnemahoning Trail (OST). That trail departs from the QT at its 39.86 mi point and heads northeast to a side street in the village of Wyside. Go a few blocks west on Jerry Run Road then turn north on Wykoff Run Road and follow it to the long bridge over Sinnemahoning Creek and then to PA 120 (a distance of about six tenths of a mile from the OST terminus). This point is just outside the village of Sinnemahoning at a tavern called Willows Inn. Turn east on PA 120 and travel three tenths of a mile (past the junction with PA 872 and the bridge over the First Fork of Sinnemahoning Creek) to Jericho Road. This junction is the western terminus of the Donut Hole Trail, which hikes east about 94 miles to Farrandsville near Lock Haven. In 2020, your present author also published a guidebook to that trail, but it is now out of print and tough to find. Watch for a new edition from Sunbury Press in the coming years.

And finally, truly obsessive hikers will be interested to learn that some portions of the Quehanna Trail have been incorporated into a proposed trek called the Pennsylvania Wilds ("PAW") Megaloop. This trek has been advocated by the Pennsylvania Wilds Center for Entrepreneurship, Keystone Trails Association, and the Department of Conservation and Natural Resources to promote ecotourism in the Pennsylvania Wilds region of north-central Pennsylvania. This loop will make use of segments of several of the region's long-distance backpacking trails, including some of the QT, plus lesser-known side trails and some newly constructed segments. The loop will traverse eight counties and is currently estimated to be a whopping 302 miles in length, and will pass through six state forests, seven state parks, and at least six towns. Watch for promotions of the PAW Megaloop in the near future.

BLAZES AND TRAIL CHARACTERISTICS

As an official Pennsylvania state forest long-distance backpacking trail, the main Quehanna Trail is marked with orange blazes throughout its distance. The blazes on the other trails described in this guide have changed color many times over the years as they are redesignated for various uses. As of the time of writing, the Cut Off Trail, West Cross Connector Trail, East Cross Connector Trail, Old Sinnemahoning Trail, and Bear Run Trail are marked with yellow blazes.

In Quehanna Wild Area, the many nearby trails can cause some confusion if you are following the yellow-blazed East Cross Connector Trail.

Many short trails in the area are also yellow-blazed. This leads to a bunch of confusing trail junctions marked by signs that hopefully will survive the ravages of time. Note that trails with blue blazes are designated for cross-country skiing, and those with red blazes are for horseback riders and mountain bikers. Hikers can use these trails as desired, but it is polite to avoid skiing trails in the winter.

In any event, the blazes are generally plentiful and easy to follow, except for a few problematic areas that are described in this guide. Sharp turns are usually denoted by double blazes and occasionally arrows. The rectangular blazes are typically painted on trees alongside the trail and are usually visible from a comfortable distance. In some treeless spots, poles have been secured in the ground to bear the blazes. Blazes are also occasionally on rocks underfoot.

ACCESS POINTS AND PARKING

Some areas of the Quehanna Trail network are very difficult to reach by car. On the southern portions of the main Quehanna Trail loop, you will hike more than 30 miles without crossing a paved road. On the northern portions of the loop, you will hike about 21 miles without crossing a paved road. The 6.27 mile-long West Cross Connector Trail does not cross a paved road. These are enormous distances for Pennsylvania.

However, there are a plethora of dirt roads in the area, some of which have official state forest parking lots. These roads, with some exceptions as noted in this guide, should be passable for most vehicles during the warm seasons, but people with small low-clearance cars must exercise extra caution. The situation is much more challenging in the winter, because the dirt roads are plowed irregularly or never, as manpower dictates. For day hikers, this will make much of the Quehanna Trail network inaccessible during the winter, especially because the Quehanna plateau region receives significantly more snow than the nearby low-lying areas.

Experienced hikers will know that other roads might have wide spots near a trail crossing where one or two cars can park. Some such possibilities are described in this guide at the applicable crossing points. However, for any road crossing that does not have an official parking lot as described below, use these access points at your own risk.

If you would like to hike in the winter, the paved roads will be plowed regularly, including Mud Run Road (at Parker Dam State Park), Quehanna Highway, Wykoff Run Road, and the numbered state highways. However, the same cannot be guaranteed for the hikers' parking lots. It would be wise to bring a shovel so you can clear out a spot.

Official state forest parking lots are accessed are as follows.

QUEHANNA TRAIL

For the main Quehanna Trail loop, these are listed counterclockwise from the starting point used in this guide.

PARKER DAM STATE PARK:

GPS LOCATION: N41° 11.681' W78° 30.388'

This is the "official" trailhead used as the starting point for this guide. Parker Dam State Park is in northern Clearfield County and is reached via PA 153. The park's access road (Mud Run Road) meets PA 153 about 2.5 miles south of the junction with PA 255 at Penfield, and about 5 miles north of the interchange with Interstate 80. From PA 153, turn east on Mud Run Road and proceed 2.3 miles to the park office. Next, turn onto Fairview Road, which leads to the official state park campground. Follow this road past the softball field (where elk have been known to hang out) and across a bridge over Laurel Run. The road then makes a sharp left turn, passes a campground parking area and a small maintenance building, then reaches another parking area next to the large "Quehanna Hiking Trail Trailhead" sign, about four tenths of a mile from the park office. If parking here overnight, alert the staff at the park office.

TYLER ROAD:

GPS LOCATION: N41° 11.210' W78° 27.768'

A small parking lot at the 3.29 mi point on the QT. From the office at Parker Dam State Park, continue on paved Mud Run Road for another 1.4 miles until it ends at unpaved Tyler Road. Turn right on Tyler Road and travel 3.2 miles to the parking lot on the left.

CALEDONIA PIKE (SOUTHEAST CROSSING):

GPS LOCATION: N41° 10.625' W78° 19.142'

A small parking lot at the 14.25 mi point on the QT, at the corner of Mineral Springs Road. This is 10.4 miles northwest from the beginning of Caledonia Pike at PA 879 outside of Karthaus. Despite serving as a long-distance route connecting PA 879 and PA 555, Caledonia Pike is a dirt road with inconsistent levels of maintenance, especially in the winter.

Note that the Quehanna Trail crosses Caledonia Pike again in its northwestern section, and the West Cross Connector Trail and Bear Run Trail cross this road as well, but none of those other crossings have approved parking spots.

LOST RUN ROAD:

GPS LOCATION: N41° 12.312' W78° 15.015'

This lot is a few hundred yards south of the spot where the QT crosses the road, at its 20.24 mi point. That spot is also the southern end of the East Cross Connector Trail. The lot is found by driving southwest from Quehanna Highway on the combined Reactor Road/Lost Run Road, then the unpaved Lost Run Road, for 4.3 miles. The lot can also be reached by driving north on Lost Run Road for 3.7 miles from Caledonia Pike.

QUEHANNA HIGHWAY (NEAR PIPER):

GPS LOCATION: N41° 11.764' W78° 09.090'

This parking lot is located 0.27 of a mile northwest of the QT, which crosses Quehanna Highway at its 30.23 mi point. The lot is at the corner of Reservoir Road, about one mile northwest of the industrial buildings in Piper.

THREE RUNS ROAD:

GPS LOCATION: N41° 14.129' W78° 06.914'

A small parking lot at the 36.83 mi point on the QT. This is 3.5 miles northeast of the corner of Three Runs Road and Quehanna Highway.

WYKOFF RUN ROAD:

GPS LOCATION: N41° 16.729' W78° 08.414'

This lot is next to the road bridge over Laurel Draft, at the 41.45 mi point on the QT. The lot is 5.2 miles northeast of Quehanna Highway and 4.7 miles southwest of PA 120 at Sinnemahoning. Wykoff Run Road is entirely paved and is plowed during the winter, though it's an extremely curvy road and extra vigilance is required during snowy conditions.

HOOVER ROAD:

GPS LOCATION: N41° 17.529' W78° 11.308'

A large parking lot used primarily by hunters, at the 44.57 mi point on the QT. Driving to this lot is not advised for smaller, less rugged vehicles. From Quehanna Highway about 2.5 miles northwest of Wykoff Run Road, turn east onto Lincoln Road. (Beware that there is a different Lincoln Road not too far from here. This is the one that starts on Quehanna Highway right next to the junction with Red Run Road.) Follow Lincoln Road east for 1.8 miles, then turn north on Hoover Road and continue 3.2 miles to the lot.

MUD LICK RUN ROAD:

GPS LOCATION: N41° 17.346' W78° 17.074'

A large parking lot within sight of the QT crossing of the road at its 52.65 mi point. From the Marion Brooks Natural Area parking lot on Quehanna Highway, head north on Losey Road, which later changes its name to Mud Lick Run Road. Watch for a right turn at the corner of Deible Road. Travel north in this fashion for a total distance of 2.0 miles.

GRANT ROAD:

GPS LOCATION: N41° 15.389' W78° 21.098'

This lot is a few hundred yards south of the spot where the QT crosses the road, at its 57.77 mi point. From Quehanna Highway, follow Grant Road north for three tenths of a mile. Do not confuse this road with the nearby Grant Trail which was built for off-road vehicles.

QUEHANNA HIGHWAY (AT HAYSTACK MOUNTAIN):

GPS LOCATION: N41° 15.971' W78° 24.052'

This large parking lot is on Quehanna Highway where the QT crosses that road for the second time, at its 62.54 mi point. The lot is 1.9 miles south of PA 555 at the village of Medix Run, on the north side of the road.

EAST CROSS CONNECTOR TRAIL

The north end of the East Cross Connector Trail is not reachable by car. There are two organized parking lots to the south. Also note that Beaver Run Wildlife Viewing Area, with plentiful parking, is about one half of a mile from this trail, via an easy old lane parallel to the dam, or a segment of the Lincoln Loop ski trail.

QUEHANNA HIGHWAY:

GPS LOCATION: N41° 15.882' W78° 15.911'

The East Cross Connector Trail crosses the road near a small parking lot. The lot is 9.8 miles southeast of PA 555 at Medix Run, and just a short distance west of the signed entrance road to Beaver Run Wildlife Viewing Area, on the north side of the road. A short side trail from the west side of the lot leads to the East Cross Connector at its 2.17 mi point.

SOUTH TERMINUS (LOST RUN ROAD):

GPS LOCATION: N41° 12.312' W78° 15.015'

This lot is also described for the Quehanna Trail above. It is a few hundred yards south of the official southern end of the East Cross Connector Trail, which is also at the QT's crossing of that road. The lot is found by driving southwest from Quehanna Highway on the combined Reactor Road/Lost Run Road, then the unpaved Lost Run Road, for 4.3 miles. The lot can also be reached by driving north on Lost Run Road for 3.7 miles from Caledonia Pike.

OLD SINNEMAHONING TRAIL

The north end of the Old Sinnemahoning Trail is in a residential area and should be accessible during the winter. The south end might not be accessible during the winter because it is on a gravel road with unreliable maintenance.

NORTH TERMINUS (WYSIDE):

GPS LOCATION: N41° 18.751' W78° 04.771'

From PA 120 at Sinnemahoning, follow Wykoff Run Road southbound, over the river and toward the village of Wyside. Immediately after a railroad track, turn east onto Jerry Run Road. Drive past some houses, cross the bridge over Wykoff Run, then reach the corner of Hardinger Street. This is about six tenths of a mile from PA 120. Do not park at the bottom of the dirt road that serves as the Old Sinnemahoning Trail; instead, park somewhere on Hardinger Street.

SOUTH TERMINUS:

GPS LOCATION: N41° 13.804' W78° 07.793'

This end of the OST is not an official parking lot, but there is a large gravel area where several cars can park. Do not park in front of the gate. This terminus is on Three Runs Road, 2.5 miles northeast of Quehanna Highway, and about one mile southwest of the QT's official parking lot on the same road.

OTHER TRAILS AND ROAD CROSSINGS

The Cut Off Trail, West Cross Connector Trail, and Bear Run Trail do not have official parking lots. The Cut Off Trail is short and crosses no roads at all. The others encounter various dirt roads, and these crossings are discussed as appropriate in the trail descriptions.

Important Information on Existing Trail Signs: Trail junctions and road crossings in the Quehanna network are often marked by post signs that denote distances to upcoming points of interest. Note that some of these signs are old and have been in place since before more recent trail relocations, making their listed distances inaccurate in the current day. Some of these signs are discussed in the trail descriptions as needed, but for most of them the listed distances should be treated as loose estimates only.

This guide is based exclusively on the on-the-ground measurements taken by the author, as described above. So please note that the measurements in this book often do not correspond to those listed on trail signs, but the measurements here can at least be considered more current.

GUIDE TO THE QUEHANNA TRAIL

This trail description begins at the trailhead parking lot on Fairview Road in Parker Dam State Park. The description begins in the southeasterly, counterclockwise direction from this starting point. See the "Logistics of the Quehanna Trail Network" chapter above for more details.

MI	KM	DESCRIPTION
0.00	0.00	This Quehanna Trail (QT) loop begins at the official "Quehanna Hiking Trail Trailhead" sign on Fairview Road near the Parker Dam State Park campground. The far end of the loop comes down the road straight ahead, from the campground. This is also the beginning of the Log Slide Trail, a state park footpath. To start QT loop as described in this guide (counterclockwise), head up the wide path away from the road and curve right past a reproduction of a log slide. The QT is marked with orange blazes. Primitive camping along the QT is not permitted for about the first half mile, because you will be within the boundaries of the state park and camping is only allowed at the official campground. If parking at the trailhead overnight, alert the staff at the state park office.
0.06	0.10	Footbridge over a small run; good water quality when flowing. Next is a deteriorating sign board denoting "A History Stone" that illustrates old dam construction techniques. Next, note the old building foundation with basement on the right.
0.24	0.39	Cross an intermittent run; not suitable for drinking.
0.43	0.69	Turn right then left at a junction with the Stumpfield Trail (a state park footpath); watch the orange QT blazes carefully. The QT soon passes out of the state park and into Moshannon State Forest.

MI	KM	DESCRIPTION
0.68	1.10	Pass to the left of a meadow that hosts several strange old multi-trunked trees. Little Laurel Run is just out of sight at the bottom of an embankment. There is nice camping in this area.
0.83	1.34	Cross a wide pipeline swath. Note how the pipeline goes under Little Laurel Run; construction workers restored the stream to something resembling its natural course. On the other side of the run, you can see damage caused by off-road vehicles.
1.23	1.98	Cross an unnamed run on rocks; good water quality. Next there is a hunting camp to the left. The QT enters a relatively flat and open area, though it is still quite rocky with some wet spots.
1.30	2.09	Turn right onto a grassy lane. (To the left, the Spurline Trail offers a pleasant walk to the northern segment of the QT at its 72.21 mi point.) After your right turn, the QT briefly follows an old railroad grade but then veers slightly to the left over some short boardwalks to avoid a chronically soggy area.
1.40	2.25	Turn left at a double blaze. After the left turn, the QT curves left again through a muddy area with several seep springs, then proceeds parallel to Little Laurel Run, upstream. The run is very picturesque in this area, with fine water quality. The QT is now following the historic Goodyear railroad grade and will continue to do so (with a few interruptions) for about the next three miles. [Seeley, 6] Back at the turn, the yellow-blazed CPL Trail goes straight ahead and heads south to S.B. Elliott State Park, following another historically notable old railroad grade operated by the Central Pennsylvania Lumber company.
1.54	2.48	Turn left at a junction with an unblazed side trail. That trail hops over a branch of Little Laurel Run then immediately dead-ends at a nice resting spot on an island in the stream.

MI	KM	DESCRIPTION
1.57	2.53	Turn left again amidst dense mountain laurel and giant rhododendron; watch the blazes carefully. Little Laurel Run is still to the right of the trail.
1.76	2.83	The trail turns right in a field of boulders.
1.90	3.06	Enter another rocky area, with possible campsites to the right alongside a particularly scenic stretch of Little Laurel Run.
1.97	3.17	Bear right onto a brief sidehill segment. You are now entering a relatively flat and sparsely forested valley that offers many possible camping locations, on both sides of the stream.
2.22	3.57	Note the field of large boulders to the right, which creates a riffle in Little Laurel Run.
2.24	3.61	Turn left onto another section of the old railroad grade. Note the severe meander in Little Laurel Run.
2.38	3.83	After a few minor detours around seep springs (not suitable for drinking), the old railroad grade enters a small treeless meadow. During my visit in mid-2025, there were several impressive beaver dams on Little Laurel Run in this area.
2.43	3.91	Trail register; please sign in.
2.50	4.03	Pass through a treeless area under a powerline. Watch for a piped spring at the bottom of the slope on the left, with excellent water quality. The blazes are on rocks underfoot; watch them carefully. Resist the urge to head straight for the road that is visible ahead and instead keep left alongside the bottom of the hill.
2.56	4.12	Turn left on Laurel Run Road and follow the road for a short distance to the next double blaze. (To the right, there are some parking spots on the far side of the road bridge over the run.)

MI	KM	DESCRIPTION
2.59	4.17	Turn right off the road onto trail. Then almost immediately turn left onto another segment of the old railroad grade and proceed roughly parallel to the road, which is on your left.
2.75	4.43	Pass behind a hunting camp. Little Laurel Run is still off in the distance to the right, surrounded by large meadows. This is another active beaver dam area.
3.05	4.91	Cross a small footbridge while surrounded by artificial drainage channels related to the construction of the old railroad grade. The QT next crosses Laurel Run Road again at an angle and continues ahead on another segment of the old railroad grade. (There is no convenient parking near this road crossing.)
3.17	5.10	Another hunting camp is visible to the left.
3.25	5.23	Cross an old woods road.
3.29	5.30	Turn right briefly on Tyler Road then turn left into a small parking lot. This is a convenient parking location for the southwestern segments of the QT.
3.33	5.36	At the back of the parking lot, walk around a vehicle gate and continue ahead on a hunting camp driveway, which was built on top of the old railroad grade.
3.41	5.49	After passing the hunting camp and a weird little clearing in which a feed basket shares space with a satellite dish, continue ahead on the old railroad grade. The grade is a pleasant grassy lane at first but quickly reverts to a footpath.
3.47	5.59	Just after a drainage ditch, reach a junction with the yellow-blazed Cut Off Trail, which heads to the left (north) for 1.68 miles to the northern section of the QT at its 71.44 mi point. The Cut Off Trail has its own description later in this book. The QT continues ahead eastbound, easily and with few curves on the old railroad grade for almost another mile.

MI	KM	DESCRIPTION
4.00	6.44	Interesting tunnel though a stand of beech trees. Note the large open meadows to the right of the trail, in a recently logged area.
4.30	6.92	Pass through a meadow with high grasses and relatively few ferns, unlike most other meadows in this region.
4.41	7.10	Emerge at the intersection of McGeorge Road and Wallace Mines Road; the latter goes straight ahead. There might be room for one or two cars to park at the corners. Bear left diagonally across the intersection and continue on a trail segment that diverges slightly away from Wallace Mines Road.
4.54	7.31	Pass a meadow on the left while climbing slightly.
4.63	7.46	Watch the blazes carefully and bear left at an apparent trail junction.
4.69	7.55	Cross the end of an old woods road, with a small hunting camp to the right.
4.82	7.76	Pass through an area with several double blazes denoting surprise turns. Watch the blazes carefully.
4.90	7.89	Turn right, with the edge of a large wetland becoming visible to your left.
4.95	7.97	Reach Wallace Mines Road, where the QT jogs left briefly then continues into the woods. The yellow-blazed West Cross Connector Trail departs to the left along the road. That trail has its own description later in this book.
5.03	8.10	Cross a footbridge over a small stream. Next, turn rapidly right then left.
5.07	8.17	Another footbridge over an intermittent run.
5.28	8.50	Turn right briefly on a grassy lane that serves a hunting camp. Just before a rickety old vehicle bridge over the Alex Branch of Trout Run, turn left and follow the creek downstream (acceptable water quality).

Signpost at the junction of the main Quehanna Trail
and the West Cross Connector Trail,
at Wallace Mines Road.

MI	KM	DESCRIPTION
5.30	8.53	Cross a small tributary stream (questionable water quality).
5.38	8.66	Cross another small tributary (poor water quality) of the Alex Branch, which is now to your right.
5.56	8.95	Pass through an especially scenic area alongside the Alex Branch. There are some possible camping spots on the other side of the stream.
5.78	9.31	Cross a muddy side channel and enter a nice camping spot.
5.91	9.52	Cross a small side stream (acceptable water quality).

MI	KM	DESCRIPTION
5.95	9.58	Turn left and begin a moderate climb away from the Alex Branch.
6.08	9.79	Pass through a hilltop meadow.
6.16	9.92	Enter another hilltop meadow, which offers some unique but dry camping opportunities. At the far edge of this meadow, there is a minor leaves-down vista to the southeast.
6.30	10.14	Cross an intermittent run in a shallow hollow and then climb briefly back to the top of the plateau.
6.43	10.35	Another hilltop meadow with a minor vista to the right.
6.50	10.47	Turn left abruptly just before a state game land boundary. Ahead, expert hikers might be able to detect an old trail that leads to an overlook. [Seeley, 7]
6.69	10.77	Begin a steep descent into Trout Hollow. The trail then levels off an old railroad grade.
6.88	11.08	Turn abruptly right off the railroad grade and head through a rocky area toward Trout Run. [Seeley, 7]
6.94	11.18	Reach a crossing of Trout Run between two noisy waterfalls. Acceptable water quality. As of 2025, a footbridge at this location was recently wiped out by a flash flood and its mangled remains are strewn about. At the time of writing, forestry officials plan to replace this bridge but at an unknown time. Until that happens, expect a knee-deep wet crossing here.
7.10	11.43	The trail joins another segment of the historic Goodyear railroad grade, slightly up the hillside above Trout Run. The trail soon passes into State Game Lands #94. No camping is allowed for the next 1.66 miles (2.68 km).
7.16	11.53	Cross a pipeline swath. Note the large boulders in this area.

MI	KM	DESCRIPTION
7.45	12.00	The trail curves broadly left (east) into Roberts Hollow, still on the old railroad grade. Roberts Run appears at the bottom of the slope to the right.
7.70	12.40	The trail is now alongside Roberts Run; acceptable water quality.
7.97	12.83	After diverging from Roberts Run a bit, watch your footing carefully through a wet area. The trail continues roughly parallel to the run.
8.22	13.24	Cross a small tributary stream; acceptable water quality.
8.30	13.37	Turn left then right; watch the blazes carefully. The trail continues roughly parallel to Roberts Run but the creek is now too far away to see (though you may still be able to hear it).
8.57	13.80	Pass through an outcropping of large boulders.
8.76	14.11	Cross the boundary out of the State Game Lands and back into Moshannon State Forest. Primitive camping is again permitted. To the left, note the long rock ledge just below the top of the hillside.
8.78	14.14	Turn left and begin a moderately strenuous, diagonal climb up the side of the hollow. The trail will level off just below the top of the plateau.
9.26	14.91	Turn right and descend back into the hollow.
9.36	15.07	Turn left and cross the high footbridge over Roberts Run (acceptable water quality). Note that this bridge is slightly downstream from a former wet crossing on rocks. [Seeley, 8] Nice camping in this area. Bear left again at the far side of the bridge.
9.44	15.19	Hop across a spring outlet that forms a little stream. Good water quality but go downstream a bit if necessary.
9.51	15.31	Hop across a tributary of Roberts Run (good water quality). Next is a steep but brief climb into a meadow on top of the plateau.

MI	KM	DESCRIPTION
9.74	15.68	Curve right on high ground above an extensive meadow complex, with several wetlands and beaver ponds in the distance to the left. Next, curve right again and begin a long but mostly gentle climb up a shallow hollow. Little happens except for quiet solitude for about the next mile.
10.78	17.36	Turn left and cross an intermittent upper tributary of Roberts Run then continue uphill. The climb gets steeper as you approach the height of land.
11.08	17.85	Cross a hunting camp driveway, after which the trail curves broadly to the left (east). Next, begin a steep but relatively brief climb up a knob on top of the plateau.
11.30	18.20	Reach a high point with a partial vista to the left. The lumpy top of this knob contains the highest point on the Quehanna Trail, at about 2400 feet elevation. There was once a failed attempt at a farming settlement at this clearly unfavorable location. [Seeley, 9]
11.69	18.83	After a gentle descent off the knob, cross a hunting camp driveway that comes in a short distance from Chestnut Ridge Road.
11.86	19.10	Cross a severely eroded old road grade during a mild descent. You will see a few more suspicious drainage channels in this otherwise nondescript area.
12.28	19.77	Cross Knobs Road. Right next to the crossing, hunters have attempted to turn a mud pit into a parking spot. Park here at your own risk; otherwise, there is no convenient parking nearby.
12.31	19.82	Note the spring-fed pond to the left (questionable water quality). In the 1930s there was a Civilian Conservation Corps camp here. They had a powerful spring that is now used by a hunting camp that is dimly visible from the trail. [Seeley, 9]
12.43	20.02	Pass through a boggy area where several springs flow forth to form the upper reaches of Deer Creek (questionable water quality).

MI	KM	DESCRIPTION
12.61	20.31	Deer Creek is now to the left of the trail (acceptable water quality).
13.09	21.08	After briefly reuniting with Deer Creek, turn right then left.
13.22	21.29	Reach Deer Creek again. There are some possible campsites in this area, though the ground is generally rocky.
13.42	21.61	Watch the blazes carefully for an abrupt left turn. Cross Deer Creek on rocks, in the midst of a pretty spot with several small waterfalls. Scramble up the embankment on the far side then turn right. The QT parallels the run again for a short distance, then soon diverges to the left to follow a small tributary upstream.
13.85	22.30	Pass through a rocky stripe near the top of the hollow, which is actually a dry watercourse where you may hear an underground run bubbling beneath the rocks.
14.16	22.80	Reach the top of the plateau in an extensive field of mountain laurel.
14.25	22.95	Turn right briefly on Caledonia Pike then turn left on Mineral Springs Road. There is a small parking lot here, with additional space for a few more cars around the road junction. Caledonia Pike was once part of an early long-distance turnpike that traveled from Bellefonte in Centre County to Smethport in McKean County. That road was opened in 1825 and even had a covered bridge over the West Branch Susquehanna River at Karthaus. Caledonia Pike was one of just two or three roads in the entire Quehanna plateau region until the early 20th Century. [Seeley, 10]
14.38	23.16	Turn right off of Mineral Springs Road and onto trail.
14.87	23.95	Turn left at a double blaze. The QT soon begins a moderate descent into Gifford Hollow.

MI	KM	DESCRIPTION
15.13	24.36	Turn left and begin a steeper descent toward Gifford Run.
15.31	24.65	In the midst of an extensive system of meadows and wetlands, cross the footbridge over Gifford Run (good water quality). There are some nice camping spots on the far side of the bridge. Next, the QT follows the boisterous Gifford Run downstream. A wide spot in the run to the right of the bridge is a remainder of a system of splash dams. The bridge is supported by much older rock walls, which were built during the logging period to manage the flow of the stream toward the splash dams. [Seeley, 10]
15.65	25.20	The trail is right alongside Gifford Run for a short distance. This segment may be difficult during times of high water.
15.69	25.27	Turn left and scramble up the embankment.
15.74	25.35	Turn left and cross a footbridge over a side stream (acceptable water quality).
16.00	25.76	Pass a great camping spot in a hollowed-out area (possibly an old quarry) across from a well-defined island in Gifford Run. Next, bear left and climb briefly away from the creekside.
16.22	26.11	Turn sharply left and climb up a minor ridgeline between Gifford Run and a side hollow.
16.54	26.64	Curve right and descend steeply.
16.57	26.68	Cross an old footbridge over a small run. Next, begin a steep but fairly brief climb to the top of the plateau.
16.71	26.91	Watch your footing carefully as you walk along the edge of a low cliff, then turn left.
17.13	27.59	Watch carefully for an abrupt left turn as a different unblazed trail continues ahead.
17.38	27.99	Turn abruptly left then right alongside a hunting camp.

MI	KM	DESCRIPTION
17.40	28.03	Turn right on Merrill Road.
17.44	28.08	In front of a hunting camp, turn left on Blue Ridge Road. This particular cabin is of historic interest. [Seeley, 11] There are some parking spots in this area, but do not park in any hunting camp's yard or driveway.
17.51	28.20	Across from another hunting camp, turn right off of Blue Ridge Road and onto trail.
17.97	28.94	Begin a moderately steep descent into Deserter Hollow.
18.08	29.11	Turn right and cross a footbridge over Deserter Run; acceptable water quality. Legend has it that this little hollow was a hideout for deserters during the Civil War and World War I. [Seeley, 12] The QT has now passed into Quehanna Wild Area. (For more details, see "Appendix B: Piper and Quehanna Wild Area.") The trail next turns left and follows the run, rising gently toward the top of the hollow.
18.43	29.68	The trail bears right at a double blaze and trends away from Deserter Run.
18.56	29.89	Turn right onto an old road grade. Confusingly, there is a QT post sign off the trail to the left of this turn. After turning right, follow the lane easily and uneventfully for the next 1.24 mi (1.99 km).
19.22	30.95	Cross a wide powerline swath at an angle. Watch carefully for the next blaze on the far side. The old lane you've been following continues ahead.
19.51	31.42	Pass through a small meadow, one of the few landmarks in this area.
19.69	31.71	Robust spring to the right of the trail, which forms a stream that flows toward a hemlock grove (questionable water quality).
19.80	31.88	Turn right abruptly onto an old railroad grade, just before a white-blazed State Game Lands boundary. Follow this grade in a nearly straight line directly east for the next 0.63 mi (1.02 km).

MI	KM	DESCRIPTION
20.24	32.59	Walk around a dirt mound that deters motorized vehicles and cross Lost Run Road. The QT continues ahead, still on the easy old grade for a while, though it soon reverts to a footpath. The yellow-blazed East Cross Connector Trail starts here and heads down the road to the left (that trail has its own description later in this book). Meanwhile there is a small parking area a few hundred yards up the road to the right. WARNING: About four miles ahead, a crucial trail bridge at Mosquito Creek was destroyed by flooding in 2011 and is still to be replaced. As of the time of writing, this is a wet river crossing that absolutely must not be attempted during high water periods. The junction with Lost Run Road here is your last chance for a detour. See "Appendix A: Mosquito Creek and Corporation Dam" for more details.
20.43	32.90	In a copse of giant rhododendron bushes, the QT curves right above the edge of Mosquito Creek Gorge.
20.63	33.22	Trail register; please sign in.
20.73	33.38	Cross a powerline swath, which offers a view down into the gorge to the left.
21.23	34.19	Partial vista from a large, flat boulder. The crease on the opposite hillside is the path of a small run that plunges toward Mosquito Creek below. You may be able to hear that creek at the bottom of the gorge, but you cannot yet see it.
21.35	34.38	The trail turns right, away from the edge of the gorge, then turns left at a dry campsite.
21.66	34.88	Pass through a meadow.

View over Mosquito Creek Gorge.

MI	KM	DESCRIPTION
21.92	35.30	Turn right along the edge of the gorge once again, then pass Wild Cat Rock, which sports a gravestone-like memorial for a hunter who allegedly killed three "wildcats" here in 1946. Ralph Seeley considers this to be a tall tale, because the hunter most likely shot a mother bobcat and two cubs—not the most impressive of achievements. Also, 1946 is probably when the memorial plaque was made, with the hunting exploit taking place years previously. [Seeley, 13]
21.95	35.35	Just before a powerline swath, there is a partial leaves-down view to the southeast toward a confluence of gorges where Gifford Run and Twelve Mile Run flow into Mosquito Creek. Next, cross the swath and bear right while passing under the power cables. Watch blazes carefully.
21.99	35.41	Just after reentering the woods, turn sharply left at a junction with the Gifford Ridge Trail and pass another leaves-down view to the right, over the aforementioned confluence of gorges. On a clear day you might be able

MI	KM	DESCRIPTION
(cont.)		to see the Allegheny Front beyond the West Branch Susquehanna River and Interstate 80, more than 25 miles from here. [Seeley, 13] The QT dips below the edge of Mosquito Creek gorge and becomes more challenging.
22.08	35.56	Turn left for a steep but brief descent. The trail then turns right onto an uneven, rock-strewn bench about two-thirds of the way up the side of the gorge. The hiking will be relatively level but surprisingly tiring due to all the rocks. Continue ahead south and southeast in this vein for the next 1.93 mi (3.10 km).
22.85	36.80	Pass a noteworthy house-sized boulder.
23.42	37.71	Pass some more house-sized boulders and a smattering of especially enormous rhododendron bushes.
24.01	38.66	Finally begin the very steep plunge toward Mosquito Creek, heading into Gifford Hollow first.
24.10	38.81	Turn sharply left, parallel to Gifford Run.

WARNING: From here to the 24.36 mi point in this guide, the route may change by the time of your visit. There have been multiple plans to relocate the Quehanna Trail to reach a variety of proposed sites for a new footbridge over Mosquito Creek. At the time of this writing in late 2025, the plan is to build a new bridge at a spot a few hundred yards upstream (north), but a schedule for doing so has not yet been confirmed. If any developments have progressed by the time of your visit, the trail is likely to become one-third to one-half of a mile longer in this area, and some of the point-by-point instructions below may become outdated.

Ahead, you will see the sites of several ill-fated bridges. This guide presents the QT as it existed at the time of my inspection in mid-2025, so below you will read about a wet crossing that absolutely must not be attempted during high water periods.

MI	KM	DESCRIPTION
(cont.)		After walking alongside Gifford Run from the 24.10 mi point as described above, you next walk across a flat area that was once at the bottom of a large artificial lake, behind by a structure called Corporation Dam that caused enormous environmental damage. For more details on the history and ecology of this area, and an explanation of what happened to the bridge, see "Appendix A: Mosquito Creek and Corporation Dam."
24.24	39.03	Continue straight ahead through the yard of a hunting camp. This camp is reached via an unstable swinging footbridge over Gifford Run to the right. Unless you're a tightrope walker, resist the urge to explore the world on the other side of this bridge.
24.29	39.11	Cross an old jeep road that once led to the hunting camp. (To the right, this road disappears under Gifford Run, with a steep cliff on the other side. How did the road continue? See Appendix A.)
24.32	39.16	Turn left alongside Mosquito Creek and cross a small side stream (poor water quality). You are likely to see signs of beaver activity in this area.
24.35	39.21	Reach the site of the most recent footbridge to cross Mosquito Creek, where you can see the former foundations on both sides of the stream. If you are here and hope to continue the Quehanna Trail, a wet crossing of this wide creek awaits. During periods of low water, it may be plausible to find a shallow spot for a knee-deep crossing. You may have to explore the banks of the creek for a while to find a viable spot. Make the usual precautions for getting wet. Do not (repeat: DO NOT) attempt to cross the creek during periods of high water, because the creek can get quite deep and the current can be very strong.

The 6′4″ author, knee-deep in Mosquito Creek
during a dry week.

MI	KM	DESCRIPTION
24.36	39.23	If you have worked your way across Mosquito Creek somewhere near the former bridge site, climb up the embankment on the other side, find the next orange blaze somewhere to the right, and continue following the QT alongside the creek downstream. In the next few minutes, you will pass the sites of two other failed footbridges over the creek.
24.43	39.34	Cross a high footbridge over Twelve Mile Run (acceptable water quality). After the bridge, bear left, hop over a line of rocks, then turn right (southeast) and continue parallel to Mosquito Creek downstream. The origin of this line of rocks is a mystery; it was probably a retaining wall along the former artificial lake to manage the flow of water toward the splash dam. [Seeley, 10]

MI	KM	DESCRIPTION
24.54	39.52	Reach an open area where you can see several flat-topped gravel embankments with nearly vertical sides. These are steep mini-canyons excavated by Mosquito Creek and Gifford Run through the soft silt of the former lakebed. Multiple channels of each stream have formed a delta-like pattern dissected by nearly vertical dirt walls with flat terrain on top. The sparsely vegetated landscape alongside Mosquito Creek in this immediate area is original and is significantly lower than the surroundings. Note the ancient tree stumps sitting many feet below the flat-topped embankments, which are themselves covered by much younger trees and brush. (See Appendix A.)
24.58	39.58	Another viewing spot for the weird mini-canyons of Mosquito Creek and Gifford Run. The long-gone Corporation Dam was located where the channels currently come back together, just downstream from the spot where Gifford Run comes in from the far side. Beavers are active in this area as well.

This deceptively benign valley along Mosquito Creek was formerly
the bottom of a ruinous artificial lake.

MI	KM	DESCRIPTION
24.63	39.66	Turn left twice and begin a long and very steep climb out of Mosquito Creek gorge.
24.68	39.74	Switchback right onto what appears to be an old tram road or log slide.
24.83	39.98	Continue climbing amongst giant house-sized boulders.
25.06	40.35	The QT has leveled off on top of the plateau, and the hiking gets much easier. For more than a mile ahead, the trail rises very gently; otherwise not much else happens.
26.19	42.17	Walk across a wide powerline swath which is signed as the Fisher Trail for snowmobiles. A fairly confusing sign here fails to mention the Quehanna Trail, but the QT continues ahead on an old forestry road that is also signed as the Mohawk Trail. The road carries both orange and red blazes. Follow this road easily and uneventfully for the next 1.98 mi (3.19 km).
26.32	42.38	Pass a vehicle gate. Coming up, you will see several jeep tracks branching off the forestry road, most marked by numbered posts. These currently go to specially reserved hunting spots for disabled persons. These tracks originated as very long hunting camp driveways traversed as early as the 1920s by wealthy weekenders in Model Ts and Model As. [Seeley, 16]
27.57	44.40	Pass a junction with the Cole Run Trail on the left. Note that the distance on the sign for Quehanna Highway is via the Mohawk Trail, not the QT.
27.83	44.81	Just before jeep track #5, to the right of the forestry road, a spring emerges from under an ancient stump to form an upper branch of Cole Run. Acceptable water quality in season.
28.17	45.36	The QT finally leaves the Mohawk Trail and turns right onto a narrower but still easy old lane. Watch the orange QT blazes carefully. (Ahead, the Mohawk Trail

MI	KM	DESCRIPTION
(cont.)		leads about 1.2 miles to Quehanna Highway northwest of the hiker's parking lot at the corner of Reservoir Road.)
29.01	46.71	At a junction with the Middle Ridge Trail, turn left onto a narrower footpath. The QT is again marked solely with orange blazes.
29.09	46.84	Cross an upper branch of Right Cole Run in a meadow; excellent water quality.
29.29	47.17	Right Cole Run itself appears to the right of the trail; excellent water quality.
29.50	47.50	Turn right, cross Right Cole Run, then turn left for a gentle ascent, still beside the stream for a while. There is a nice campsite up a little side trail just before the crossing.
29.81	48.00	Hop across a seasonal trickle of water—the extreme upper source of the Cole Run watershed (poor water quality up here). Next, climb up a minor ridgeline with a very large meadow to the right.
30.13	48.52	Pass through a dark grove of hemlock trees, which appear to have been planted in a stripe as a visual buffer parallel to Quehanna Highway.
30.23	48.68	Cross Quehanna Highway and head toward a post sign on the far side. Note that the speed limit is 55 mph. Do not park at this crossing; there is an official hikers' parking lot 0.27 mi (0.43 km) down the road to the left, at the corner of Reservoir Road. The Quehanna Trail next enters a young forest that has grown since a previous forest was clear-cut after a ruinous insect infestation. [Seeley, 16] Piper is about half a mile up the road to the right. There are no services for hikers in Piper; this so-called "town" is actually just a small collection of industrial buildings and a low-security prison. For more details, see "Appendix B: Piper and Quehanna Wild Area."

MI	KM	DESCRIPTION
(cont.)		NOTE: If you are hiking in the other direction, Quehanna Highway is your last viable bail-out point before a bridgeless crossing of Mosquito Creek about six miles to the west. For more details, see "Appendix A: Mosquito Creek and Corporation Dam."
30.43	49.00	Watch the blazes carefully for a couple of surprise turns. It was difficult to build a more straightforward path in this area due to the densely packed young trees.
30.61	49.29	Hop over an ancient road grade at the edge of a large meadow. Enter a more mature forest.
30.70	49.44	Note the powerful spring to the right; this is actually an underground stream that emerges and forms the upper reaches of Rider Draft. Good water quality. In the Quehanna plateau region you will occasionally see the peculiar term "Draft" for what is called a "Run" everywhere else. The origins of this term are obscure, but it is probably a local nickname for a hollow with a certain configuration that creates a cool breeze. [Seeley, 17]
30.90	49.76	Turn left briefly under a powerline, then turn right into the woods. Watch blazes carefully. The QT next climbs moderately up a knob on top of the plateau.
31.01	49.94	The trail levels off in an area of dense mountain laurel and sparse trees. There are some partial views over the rolling plateau landscape to the right.
31.06	50.02	Begin a mild descent through a system of large meadows, with more plateau views straight ahead.
31.19	50.23	Turn sharply left along the edge of a shallow valley. Watch the blazes very carefully, because there are few of them in this area due to the shortage of trees.
31.31	50.42	Cross an intermittent run and head upstream. Questionable water quality even in season.

Giant rhododendron bushes blooming along the
trail in late June, near Piper.

MI	KM	DESCRIPTION
31.45	50.64	Turn left briefly at a powerline swath then turn right back into the woods. There are some red blazes for horseback riders here that could cause confusion; watch for the orange QT blazes carefully.
31.48	50.69	Cross a different powerline swath and continue straight ahead.
31.98	51.50	Begin a steep descent into Upper Three Runs Hollow.
32.16	51.79	Cross an old road grade and continue descending. A short distance ahead, note the springs popping up out of the hillside, forming an intermittent stream. Acceptable water quality when flowing.

MI	KM	DESCRIPTION
32.23	51.90	Cross the aforementioned stream and continue descending steeply. You will cross the stream a couple more times on the way down the hollow.
32.50	52.33	Shuffle slightly to the right on Reservoir Road then continue into the woods. Do not attempt to reach this crossing by car because the road is gated about half a mile to the left, and it is a dead end in the other direction. Also, ignore the sign at this crossing that points to some nearby "camp sites"—those are private sites.
32.53	52.38	Cross a rather shaky bridge over the oddly named Upper Three Runs Run. Continue straight ahead for a short distance then turn sharply right.
32.74	52.72	Turn left and begin climbing up a side hollow.
33.12	53.33	Turn right, cross Laurel Swamp Draft, then continue upstream.
33.18	53.42	Cross the run again.
33.21	53.47	Curve left and begin a much steeper climb up the side of the hollow.
33.29	53.61	Turn left at an old trail junction and keep climbing, though less steeply. The trail then levels off for a while on a bench slightly below the top of the ridge.
33.46	53.88	Bear right and climb some more toward the top of the plateau. There are some leaves-down views in this area.
33.55	54.03	Pass a former vista to the south that has become overgrown; again, there may be a better view when the leaves are down in the winter.
33.60	54.11	Reach a much better vista over the hollow to the southwest. The trail soon levels off and curves right.
33.79	54.41	Turn left abruptly at a double blaze.
33.91	54.61	Turn left again onto what might be an old road grade, in a generally nondescript area.

MI	KM	DESCRIPTION
34.00	54.75	Turn right onto a better-defined old grade. The hiking remains easy—just watch the blazes carefully.
34.05	54.83	Turn left abruptly onto trail.
34.64	55.78	Enter an incongruous patch of hemlocks.
34.68	55.85	Boardwalk through a swampy spot caused by several seep springs, which form the headwaters of Laurel Swamp Draft. The extra water supports the hemlocks, which are not often seen in flat hilltop areas like this.
34.88	56.17	Reach a large meadow on top of the plateau, then turn left onto a spur of Three Runs Tower Road. There are extensive meadows in all directions. At some high spots in this area, to the east you can see the similar high plateau landscape beyond the West Branch Susquehanna River, between Renovo and Snow Shoe. There is another long-distance backpacking trail in that area: the 50+ mile Chuck Keiper Trail. Guidebooks for that trail are in the bailiwick of expert Pennsylvania hiker Dave Gantz; watch for a new edition from Sunbury Press in 2026 or 2027.
35.00	56.36	At a road junction, continue straight ahead on a grassy jeep lane. Pass the site of an old fire tower and the ruins of its cabin on the left, then walk through a pleasant but dry campsite.
35.05	56.43	Pass a junction with the #14 Trail on the left. Continue following an old jeep road for the next 0.16 mi (0.27 km).
35.21	56.70	Watch carefully for an abrupt right turn off the road and onto a footpath.
35.26	56.78	Cross a grassy lane.
35.31	56.86	Cross a wide grassy swath that connects massive meadows on both sides. This is prime elk territory.
35.63	57.37	Turn left twice and descend, first through a very rocky zone.

MI	KM	DESCRIPTION
35.73	57.54	Pass a partial vista to the right.
36.07	58.09	Bear right and descend into a hemlock-heavy area.
36.13	58.17	You may see an old springhouse below the trail to the right, with water flowing down a wooden sluice (excellent water quality). Next, curve right toward the bottom of the hollow.
36.14	58.20	Cross an upper tributary of Lower Three Runs Run. During wet periods this creek begins some distance to your left and flows straight through this spot; during dry periods it may begin here by emerging from a spring under a tree. Excellent water quality. Next, curve left through a great camping spot.
36.42	58.64	Turn right (north) at a junction with the #15 Trail. Join an old woods road that heads gently uphill.
36.69	59.08	Pass to the left of a large meadow.
36.80	59.27	Bear left at a fork in the old lane.
36.83	59.31	Cross Three Runs Road and walk through a parking lot. Please sign in at the trail register. The QT continues northbound beyond the lot.
37.28	60.03	Skirt the edge of a large meadow.
37.56	60.48	Upper Jerry Run appears to the right of the trail, in an area that is generally favorable for camping. Water quality in the run is questionable up here but will improve downstream.
37.81	60.89	Hop across Upper Jerry Run carefully then climb up the bank on the far side. The trail then turns left into a meadow.
37.91	61.05	Watch the blazes carefully for some surprise turns in an area of dense hemlocks.
38.24	61.58	Reach the run again in a nice but cramped camping spot, then turn right.

MI	KM	DESCRIPTION
38.47	61.95	Cross an intermittent stream fed by a spring under a boulder to the right. Good water quality in season. The trail is still parallel to Upper Jerry Run.
38.50	62.00	Cross another tributary stream coming down the hillside; good water quality in season. The hiking is pleasant alongside Upper Jerry Run, with some possible camping spots here and there.
38.76	62.42	Cross a side channel of the run as best you can. This crossing will be a challenge during high water. There are two more troublesome crossings ahead.
38.97	62.75	At an old pipeline apparatus, turn left and cross Upper Jerry Run for the final time at another very challenging spot. Prepare to get wet during high water periods. The trail next begins a steep climb up a side hollow.
39.00	62.80	Cross the side hollow's rapidly plunging stream (good water quality) and continue climbing steeply.
39.14	63.03	About two-thirds of the way up the hollow, the run is now underground, and you may hear it bubbling beneath your feet. The struggle continues all the way to the height of land.
39.29	63.27	After a relentless climb, the trail finally levels off on top of the plateau.
39.43	63.49	Walk through a row of boulders (apparently a vehicle barrier), then bear right along the edge of an extensive meadow that is being managed as a feed lot for wildlife. You will soon cross this meadow, so watch carefully for the orange blazes on faraway trees.
39.56	63.70	Bear left as the meadow narrows to the dimensions of a wide grassy lane.
39.62	63.80	At a four-way intersection of grassy lanes, turn right. There are even more meadows ahead, which are being managed to attract elk. You will also see extensive vernal pools in the spring. The lane onto which you have

MI	KM	DESCRIPTION
(cont.)		just turned is the Old Sinnemahoning Trail (OST), which has its own description later in this book. The two trails are concurrent for the next 0.24 mi (0.39 km).
39.86	64.19	Watch carefully for an abrupt left turn off the old lane and onto a narrower footpath, which will carry the QT into Upper Pine Hollow. (Ahead, the yellow-blazed OST continues on the grassy lane and eventually reaches the village of Wyside near Sinnemahoning Creek.)
39.94	64.32	Pond to the left, where the author heard (but failed to see) what sounded like dozens of bullfrogs.
40.30	64.90	Turn left and drop into a shallow hollow that carries the highest reaches of Upper Pine Run.
40.34	64.96	Cross a watercourse that is dry most of the year. The trail heads diagonally to the right.
40.39	65.04	Pass through a soggy area formed by several seep springs, not suitable for drinking. You will see Upper Pine Run forming to your right. There are some possible camping opportunities in this area, though it might be tough to find a flat spot.
40.44	65.12	Cross the stream twice. Depending on the season, it will be either intermittent or flowing in this area, with acceptable water quality. The stream and trail are now descending rather steeply.
40.54	65.28	After a copse of enormous rhododendron bushes, cross Upper Pine Run again. The terrain is getting much rockier. (If you are hiking in the other direction, this is probably the steepest climb on the QT.)
40.68	65.51	Turn left, cross the run again, and continue downstream. There are two more crossings coming soon.
40.83	65.75	Yet another crossing of the run, after which the QT rises briefly onto an embankment above the stream.

MI	KM	DESCRIPTION
41.07	66.14	There are a few noteworthy springs in this area, with good water quality in season. After briefly walking alongside Upper Pine Run again, the trail joins what appears to be an ancient railroad grade, keeping a relatively stable elevation above the stream for a while.
41.25	66.43	Turn left and head back toward the bottom of the hollow.
41.29	66.49	Turn right into a possible camping spot.
41.33	66.55	Cross the long footbridge over Wykoff Run. Note the extension on the far side, which became necessary when the creek rerouted itself around the former west end of the bridge, resulting in stairs that dropped into the water. [Seeley, 22] Next, turn right, parallel to Wykoff Run Road. Due to the proximity of the road, no camping is allowed in this area
41.42	66.70	Watch the blazes carefully as the trail bears left then right. To the left, you may see an old building foundation below Wykoff Run Road.
41.45	66.75	Emerge at a state forest parking lot on Wykoff Run Road. The QT next turns briefly right on the road and crosses the bridge over Laurel Draft. This is one of the lowest points on the QT, surrounded by extensive elevation gains in both directions. You just completed one in the downhill direction, so brace yourself for what comes next.
41.48	66.80	At the end of the guardrail on the left side of the road, turn left onto a footpath. Blazes are sparse in this area but the footpath heading up Laurel Draft is pretty obvious.
41.72	67.18	Pass a spring catchment basin; good water quality in season.
41.90	67.47	Bear right onto a more rugged trail that rises partway up the side of the canyon. Begin a long, moderately strenuous climb up Laurel Draft toward the top of

MI	KM	DESCRIPTION
(cont.)		the plateau. On the way up, you will see several nice campsites back down along the stream. Continue in this vein for the next 1.32 mi (2.13 km). In terms of elevation gain this is the most extensive climb on the entire QT when hiked in this direction, though it is long and drawn-out, and not excessively steep.
43.22	69.60	The trail levels off in a thinly forested area, with a lot of barberry (an invasive species) and huckleberry in the understory.
43.40	69.89	Turn left at a nice campsite and cross the footbridge over Laurel Draft (a good water source). The trail next climbs up a minor ridgeline. Watch the blazes carefully.
43.54	70.11	Cross a double pipeline/powerline swath, angling slightly to the left while doing so.
43.72	70.40	Cross an upper branch of Laurel Draft in a meadow. The water quality up here is still acceptable, but not during dry periods. On a previous trip, the author saw a bear in this area.
43.99	70.84	Large spring to the left; the origin of Laurel Draft. Questionable water quality.
44.12	71.05	Bear left at an obscure trail junction.
44.57	71.77	Cross Hoover Road, with a parking lot to your right. At the time of writing, the drive on Hoover Road to this spot is a struggle for smaller cars. Pass a map board and continue ahead on an old lane.
45.09	72.61	Cross a metal footbridge over an upper branch of Little Fork Run. Good water quality when flowing.
45.39	73.09	The deep Little Fork Hollow, with a loud stream somewhere at the bottom, suddenly appears on the right. There are some leaves-down views in this area.

MI	KM	DESCRIPTION
45.75	73.67	Reach Little Fork Vista. A short side trail leads down to an additional viewing spot. This is one of the premier vistas in the QT network, though at the time of writing it was getting a bit overgrown.
45.99	74.06	Cross an upper branch of Little Fork Run (acceptable water quality when flowing), then turn left and climb out of a shallow hollow. Note the ruins of two buildings on the right—an intriguing campsite. The ruins are what's left of an old farm believed to have been operated by a man named Archie Barr, who gave it a go in this unlikely area. [Seeley, 23] Next, the trail turns left again onto what remains of an old road that led to the buildings.
46.10	74.24	Bear left alongside a grove of eye-catching white birch trees. You are now on a rather wide road grade, which you will follow uneventfully for the next 0.77 mi (1.24 km). The grade is roughly level at first but then begins a long, mild descent.

What's left of Archie Barr's farmstead.

MI	KM	DESCRIPTION
46.87	75.48	Reach a complex intersection of three grassy lanes and a footpath. Ignore the yellow-blazed Sanders Ski Trail that goes diagonally left. Instead, bear right (southwest) onto a footpath that heads into a dense, mature forest. Watch the orange blazes carefully. Begin a long, gradual descent into the top of Sanders Draft.
47.19	75.98	Enter a dense rhododendron jungle. This shrub is endemic all the way down Sanders Draft, and you will pick your way through several jungles like this one. This rapidly growing shrub, in such prodigious numbers, creates a serious challenge for trail maintainers in this area.
47.22	76.04	Cross an upper segment of Sanders Draft as it pokes its way through the jungle. Acceptable water quality if flowing.
47.32	76.20	Scramble into and out of a deeply entrenched dry run. Continue down the rugged hollow and tackle its many rhododendron thickets for the next 1.22 mi (1.96 km). Sanders Draft will always be a short distance to your right, but on several occasions, you will have to climb up and around tight spots in the hollow.
48.50	78.10	Reach a fairly open area within a fork of the hollow, with some possible camping spots.
48.54	78.16	Cross a weakening split log bridge (which may have been replaced by the time of your visit) over Sanders Draft, then turn left and continue downstream.
48.67	78.37	Pass through a clutch of large boulders and reach the side of Sanders Draft again, in an area where the boulders form several small waterfalls and riffles. Ahead, the QT again has a hard time staying level. Sometimes you have a bucolic (if rocky) walk along the stream, but at other times you must climb partway up the right side of the hollow to get around tight spots.

Boulders in Sanders Draft create many
scenic waterfalls and riffles.

MI	KM	DESCRIPTION
48.90	78.74	The trail has flattened out, a bit removed from Sanders Draft. There are some possible campsites between the creek and trail.
48.97	78.86	Cross an intermittent run coming down the hillside and continue on relatively high ground.
49.17	79.18	Begin a steep descent with several sharp turns toward Red Run.
49.24	79.29	Cross the long footbridge over Red Run. Please sign in at the trail register at the far end. The QT then bears right and starts to ascend.
49.28	79.36	Turn right, downhill, on Red Run Road. Follow this road for the next 0.46 mi (0.74 km). (If you are going in the other direction, watch for this turn very

MI	KM	DESCRIPTION
(cont.)		carefully; you have missed it if the road starts to rise significantly above the creek.) There are some parking spots along the road, and it appears that many people engage in car camping in this area.
49.74	80.10	Just before the road bridge over the creek, turn left off the road and onto a grassy lane. This track remains roughly parallel to Red Run but will soon rise above it.
49.80	80.19	Cross a muddy streamlet, not suitable for drinking.
50.07	80.63	The trail curves broadly to the left into Porcupine Draft, with the run of the same name on your right. There are some nice camping spots between the trail and the run.
50.26	80.93	Make the first of five wet crossings of Porcupine Draft. This one could be tricky during high water. The run has acceptable water quality. Climb steeply up the ridgeline on the opposite side. The trail levels off briefly but then continues on a very long and drawn-out climb up Porcupine Draft. You will be climbing steadily, sometimes easily and sometimes much less easily, for the next 1.41 mi (2.27 km).
50.35	81.08	Step across a couple of intermittent streams coming down the hillside, then pass a four-foot waterfall in Porcupine Draft.
50.40	81.16	Second crossing of the run, after which the climbing gets steeper.
50.51	81.34	The trail crosses the run a third time, at an especially scenic spot where a jumble of boulders has created several small waterfalls. Next, the trail turns left and slabs part of the way up the side of the hollow.
50.60	81.48	Cross an intermittent tributary stream; not suitable for drinking.
50.69	81.63	Fourth crossing of the run, followed by an especially steep excursion up the hillside.

MI	KM	DESCRIPTION
50.92	82.00	Fifth crossing of the run. This one has steep scrambles into and out of the drink.
51.01	82.14	About two-thirds of the way up the hollow, cross the watercourse a couple more times, though the run is intermittent up here.
51.10	82.29	Cross the usually dry bed of a tributary stream, at a fork in the hollow. The trail then slowly curves into the right branch of the hollow and soon begins climbing much more steeply up the side of the canyon.
51.33	82.66	Cross a dry run, then scramble up and around one last rocky ridgeline. The toughest part of the climb is over, but the landscape continues to rise gently.
51.67	83.20	Turn left onto the one-lane Losey Road. Do not try to drive to this point because the road is gated about three-quarters of a mile south of here.
51.70	83.25	Turn right off the dirt road and onto trail. The QT has finally leveled off on top of the plateau above Porcupine Draft. (Meanwhile, the yellow-blazed East Cross Connector Trail begins here and heads straight ahead down the dirt road, southbound.)
51.98	83.70	Enter a boot-busting rocky zone with many interesting jumbles of large boulders. Next, the QT descends moderately and passes out of Quehanna Wild Area, re-entering Moshannon State Forest.
52.40	84.38	Cross two rocky low points at the top of a shallow hollow, separated by about 90 yards. After the second, begin a moderate climb to the top of the plateau.
52.47	84.49	Switchback left on the way up a ridgeline.
52.65	84.79	Cross Mud Lick Run Road, with a large parking lot to the right. Immediately after crossing the road, turn left on a grassy lane. A little later, note the water hose on the ground that serves some nearby hunting camps.

MI	KM	DESCRIPTION
(cont.)		In this area, the QT proceeds a short distance to the north of Marion Brooks Natural Area, in which no development is permitted. The tract is named after a notable local conservationist and contains what is believed to be the largest stand of white birch trees in the eastern United States. Not even hiking trails are allowed inside the natural area, though various yellow-blazed trails and old dirt roads skirt its edges. [Seeley, 25-26]
52.91	85.20	Pass between some large boulders, after which a very deep branch of Mix Hollow drops away to the right.
53.24	85.73	Bear right and descend into a side hollow. The trail becomes very rocky.
53.48	86.12	Cross a couple of intermittent runs.
53.55	86.23	Near a section of exposed pipeline that is visible ahead, turn left and begin climbing out of the side hollow.
53.82	86.67	Just after crossing an old grassy lane, cross an unnamed spur of Deible Road. A road junction where a few cars can park is just uphill to the left. This parking location can be reached in two different ways. Rugged, high-clearance vehicles could start at the Forestry building on Quehanna Highway and drive north on Deible Road. Other cars can approach via Losey Road northbound then Deible Road westbound.
53.85	86.71	Turn right onto a wide pipeline swath. Note the sign commemorating a Boy Scout troop that helped maintain the trail in this area in 2005.
53.94	86.86	Turn left abruptly onto a narrower footpath. Watch the blazes carefully.
54.19	87.26	Walk by some house-sized boulders.
54.34	87.50	Pass a large spring that forms an extreme upper tributary of Mix Run. Good water quality when flowing.

MI	KM	DESCRIPTION
54.39	87.58	Bear right at a junction with the Mosquito Creek Trail.
54.46	87.70	Begin a very steep descent into Deible Hollow. You will pass a couple a partial vistas where old windstorms created small open areas.
54.53	87.81	Switchback right at another partial vista and continue the treacherous descent.
54.61	87.94	The trail curves left into a side hollow, paralleling its run downstream. Watch the blazes carefully. The run is usually dry in this immediate area.
54.71	88.10	Cross Deible Run then turn right, downstream. Acceptable water quality. (A post sign at this turn indicates a "high water detour" that is no longer relevant due to some recent trail relocations.)
54.83	88.29	Cross Deible Run again; this crossing might be tricky during high water.
54.90	88.41	Third crossing of Deible Run. There are some camping spots in this area.

The trail alongside the deep Deible Hollow.

MI	KM	DESCRIPTION
55.09	88.71	Reach a nice camping area in a bottomland that is heavy with hemlock and giant rhododendron. Just before reaching some backwater channels of Mix Run, turn left onto an old railroad grade. The QT parallels Mix Run, upstream. Tom Mix, a superstar of westerns during the silent movie era, was born in this area in 1880 and the run was named after an ancestor who first settled in the hollow. Mix's official showbiz biography claimed that he was born in El Paso, Texas, which apparently is more believable for a silver-screen cowboy.
55.26	88.99	Cross the first footbridge over Mix Run. This run has acceptable water quality here and upstream, and the hollow contains many nice camping spots. Mix Run is a designated trout stream. In addition to great fishing, there are state regulations on bridge construction, which created additional challenges when several footbridges were built along this stream in the 1990s. [Seeley, 27]
55.53	89.42	Cross another footbridge over Mix Run and continue upstream.
55.61	89.55	The trail skirts the edge of a soggy meadow. Next, turn left then right as the trail hugs the bottom of the hillside in order to avoid some swampy bottomland.
55.88	89.98	After coming down off a sidehill segment, the trail joins another section of the old railroad grade and is alongside Mix Run again. Beware of wet spots caused by seep springs. This is another fine area for camping, on either side of the stream.
56.07	90.29	Squeeze around a small landslide that took most of the old grade with it. Watch your footing carefully.
56.14	90.40	Turn right, hop across a side channel at the site of an old railroad bridge, then turn left to rejoin the old grade.

MI	KM	DESCRIPTION
56.21	90.52	Cross the third footbridge over Mix Run, after which the trail goes straight ahead uphill for a short distance, then turns left on another segment of the old railroad grade.
56.37	90.77	The trail curves left and hops over a muddy backwater channel. More good camping in this area.
56.63	91.19	Pass through the yard of a hunting camp, cross an older footbridge over Mix Run, then turn right.
56.84	91.53	Cross an incoming tributary stream (acceptable water quality) and continue following Mix Run upstream.
56.95	91.71	Cross the run on a short split-log bridge.
57.01	91.80	Turn right into an area of dense mountain laurel and rhododendron.
57.05	91.87	Cross an intermittent run coming down the hillside (questionable water quality).
57.08	91.92	The QT is now following a rapidly plunging upper branch of Mix Run and begins a mild climb toward the top of the plateau.
57.32	92.30	Diverge to the right, away from the stream, then cross a pipeline swath and head up a minor ridgeline.
57.63	92.80	After the trail has leveled off on top of the plateau, cross another old pipeline swath.
57.77	93.03	Cross Grant Road, with a parking lot a few minutes' walk to the left. The QT continues ahead on an old woods lane, which soon peters out and reverts to a footpath. To the right (north), Grant Road eventually leads to the village of Grant on PA 555 though it is dilapidated and closed to vehicles not too far ahead. The village was named in honor of President Ulysses S. Grant, who once passed through during a fishing trip on Mix Run. He probably relaxed while his lackeys did the real fishing. [Seeley, 28]

MI	KM	DESCRIPTION
58.06	93.49	Jog left briefly on an active pipeline swath, then turn right into the woods. Watch blazes carefully.
58.34	93.95	Cross another old pipeline swath in a soggy area.
58.40	94.04	Cross a murky upper tributary of Sullivan Run on an ancient footbridge. Poor water quality. In this area you may hear vehicles on Quehanna Highway, which is about a third of a mile to the left (south).
58.78	94.65	Cross a muddy intermittent run. There are some possible camping spots in this area.
58.94	94.91	Turn right on a recent logging road.
58.98	94.97	At a vehicle turn-around spot, bear left onto a narrower footpath.
59.27	95.45	Cross a white-blazed State Game Lands boundary. The QT passes through a small slice of SGL #34; no camping is allowed for the next 0.12 mi (0.18 km). The trail is now descending into Sliver Mill Hollow on a rocky old railroad grade. Note that many maps misspell this stream and hollow as "Silver Mill" as in the precious metal. Sorry but there are no vast riches to be found around here unless you're a modern logger. Instead, the area is named after a sliver mill that once existed downstream during the early logging era. This facility processed small pieces of wood that had been rejected by logging companies—then known as "slivers"—into kindling for use in stoves. [Seeley, 28]
59.39	95.63	Cross the white-blazed boundary again (the blazes face the other way) and exit SGL #34.
59.54	95.88	Turn abruptly left off the old grade and head toward the rocky bottom of the hollow.
59.94	96.52	The trail curves right, crosses a usually dry watercourse, and continues down the rugged hollow. A sharp trench formed by Sliver Mill Run becomes visible to your right.

MI	KM	DESCRIPTION
60.31	97.12	Curve sharply left just above Sliver Mill Run. This run usually flows feebly but it somehow dug a very deep trench into the landscape. This is an indicator of periodic and destructive flash floods.
60.38	97.23	Cross two channels of an intermittent tributary stream.
60.52	97.45	After briefly walking alongside Sliver Mill Run, cross another intermittent tributary then head back toward the left side of this unusually wide hollow.
60.68	97.71	Cross another intermittent side stream. Begin a long diagonal slab up the hillside to the left. This is Haystack Mountain, the top of which is one of the highest points in this region of the Quehanna plateau. Unlike most of the other climbs in the QT network, this time the trail does not drag you all the way to the top.
61.11	98.41	If the leaves are down, there is a partial vista to the north over Sliver Mill Hollow. The trail makes a broad curve to the left (southwest) and has settled onto a somewhat level bench about halfway up the side of Haystack Mountain.
61.50	99.03	Pass some large boulders and a seasonal spring (not suitable for drinking). The trail has been descending gently for a while, and a large green field becomes visible at the bottom of the slope to the right.
61.62	99.23	Scramble down an embankment, turn left (uphill) on a steep pipeline swath, then immediately turn right back into the woods. Watch blazes carefully. Also, in this area you can hear cars on Quehanna Highway and the boisterous waters of Medix Run far below.
61.90	99.68	Cross another ridiculously steep pipeline swath. This one was abandoned long ago, and an old valve is visible just downhill to the right. You can now see Quehanna Highway down in the valley.
61.95	99.76	Bear right onto a mossy old grade, which shows evidence of past use as both a maintenance road and as a pipeline swath. Note the two different levels, which

MI	KM	DESCRIPTION
(cont.)		probably carried parallel pipelines operated by different companies.
62.05	99.92	Just before the old road begins a steep descent, bear left off the grade and onto trail. Watch blazes carefully. Note how the hillside to the left is almost entirely covered with moss.
62.14	100.06	Turn right and cross a small run; good water quality when flowing.
62.43	100.53	Trail register; please sign in. Next, bear right and cross under the high-voltage powerlines at a wide angle, keeping a parking lot to your right.
62.49	100.63	Make a U-turn to the right, scramble down a steep embankment to an old road grade, then turn left into the state forest parking lot.
62.54	100.71	From the parking lot, cross Quehanna Highway carefully (speed limit is 55 mph). On the other side, step through a gap in the guardrail then cross a footbridge over Sullivan Run. This is the lowest point on the Quehanna Trail at about 1200 feet elevation.
62.58	100.77	After a brief flat area, turn right and begin to slab up the hillside on an expertly constructed sidehill trail. Continue in a wide arc around the end of a ridge for the next 0.62 mi (1.00 km).
63.20	101.77	After a descent, you are now in a relatively flat area parallel to Medix Grade Road.
63.27	101.88	Bear left onto an old pipeline swath near a hunting camp.
63.34	102.00	Bear left off the swath and cross a small run (questionable water quality) at a spot where it disappears under a pile of rocks. Next, turn left onto a sidehill segment.
63.39	102.08	Switchback to the right and climb steeply.
63.41	102.11	After rounding a corner, continue ahead on another segment of the old pipeline swath.

MI	KM	DESCRIPTION
63.64	102.48	Pass a junction with the yellow-blazed Bear Run Trail on the right. The QT continues south on the pipeline grade. The Bear Run Trail, which is described later in this book, is a former route of the QT which was demoted due to a series of failed footbridges over Medix Run. For more details, see "Appendix C: Medix Run and the Bear Run Trail."
63.76	102.68	Walk along the left side of a large meadow that covers a natural gas drilling area, with vent pipe.
63.80	102.74	Bear left at a fork in the grassy lane.
63.84	102.80	Pass two metal boxes that conceal pipeline valves.
64.08	103.18	Note that the pipeline swath now has two levels, probably due to competing companies sharing the right-of-way. Hop left and rise briefly to the higher level.
64.24	103.45	Bear left on a driveway that comes up from Medix Grade Road. Rise briefly to a meadow with a couple of rustic shacks that house both old and new pipeline equipment.
64.34	103.60	Curve left in another meadow and climb steeply, still on the pipeline swath.
64.45	103.78	Level off and walk along the right edge of yet another large meadow with vent pipe. Rejoin the pipeline swath on the far side.
64.62	104.06	Bear right and descend steeply.
64.72	104.22	Turn left on Medix Grade Road.
64.76	104.28	Pass a historic Civilian Conservation Corps site on the left, then cross the county line (entering Clearfield County). Next, pass a large sign denoting a stream restoration project on Medix Run.
64.84	104.41	Turn right onto Little Medix Road then cross the road bridge over Medix Run. Stay on this road for next 0.52 mi (0.84 km).

MI	KM	DESCRIPTION
65.14	104.89	Reach a junction with the West Cross Connector Trail (QTWCC) which comes down the hill from the left. Continue on Little Medix Road. There are a few parking spots ahead.
65.31	105.17	Road bridge over Little Medix Run.
65.36	105.25	A few dozen yards after a double blaze on the last available telephone pole, bear right off Little Medix Road onto an old driveway. At the time of writing, a post sign at this turn incorrectly mentions the QTWCC because it was manufactured before the QT was rerouted into this area in 2016.
65.39	105.30	At what appears to be an old gas well site, turn right onto trail.
65.41	105.33	Cross a small stream (good water quality when flowing), turn right, then turn sharply left and begin a moderate climb toward the top of the plateau.
65.47	105.42	Scramble up to a pipeline swath, cross it at an angle, and continue uphill on trail. Watch blazes carefully. There are some slim possibilities for camping in this area.
65.69	105.78	About halfway up the hollow, the climb has become noticeably steeper. Note the increasingly rocky nature of the hollow as you ascend.
65.86	106.05	Turn left at a double blaze near the top of the hollow.
65.93	106.16	Begin a very steep but brief climb up a minor ridgeline. At the top, a lonely outhouse is visible to the right. The trail then levels off on top of the plateau.
66.10	106.44	Jog right very briefly on Caledonia Pike then continue into the woods. This is the second time the QT crosses Caledonia Pike. There is a possible parking spot to the right (north) of this crossing.
66.20	106.60	Cross a pipeline swath.

MI	KM	DESCRIPTION
66.34	106.82	Bear left briefly onto an old woods road, then turn right back onto trail.
66.52	107.11	Pass through a large meadow.
66.68	107.37	A hunting camp is visible to the left.
66.95	107.81	Turn abruptly left at a double blaze. The trail is now above a hollow formed by a small tributary of Laurel Run.
67.03	107.94	Enter an area with many double blazes that denote sharp turns. Watch blazes carefully.
67.48	108.66	After an easy descent into the top of a side hollow, turn sharply left into the hollow and begin a slightly steeper descent towards its bottom.
67.61	108.87	Pass by some large boulders as the trail gets rockier and steeper, passing through fairly dense mountain laurel and occasional giant rhododendron.
67.76	109.11	Cross a footbridge over an unnamed tributary of Laurel Run (acceptable water quality), then turn right into this run's hollow and follow it downstream. There are some possible camping spots near this turn. You are entering an especially pretty, steep-sided hollow. As you proceed downstream, note the massive concentrations of giant rhododendron on the slope to the left, while the slope to the right is largely devoid of shrubbery except for some sparse mountain laurel near the top. This hollow is oriented almost perfectly east-west, so the two slopes receive dramatically different amounts of sunlight as the seasons progress. This accounts for the differences in plant cover.
68.08	109.63	Cross another footbridge over the run, though the water is mostly underground at this point, and continue downstream.
68.18	109.79	Pass a small hunting camp on the left.

A great spot for a break alongside a stream that deserves
a name of its own.

MI	KM	DESCRIPTION
68.25	109.90	After some wet spots and a footbridge over a small side stream, scramble up to Saunders Road and turn left. There is no convenient parking in this area. (The Bear Run Trail departs along the road to the right.) Follow Saunders Road southbound for the next 0.80 mi (1.29 km).
68.95	111.03	After a long relatively straight section, the road crosses a pipeline swath just before a curve to the left.
69.00	111.11	Excellent piped spring on the left, across from a hunting camp.
69.05	111.19	Bear right off Saunders Road and onto a hunting camp driveway (address: 2122). Continue straight ahead at the next driveway junction. Saunders Run is now to your right.
69.12	111.30	Where the driveway turns sharply left, continue straight ahead on an old grassy lane.

MI	KM	DESCRIPTION
69.14	111.34	Cross a footbridge over Little Saunders Run (good water quality, assuming the hunting camp's propane tank isn't leaky) and continue ahead on the overgrown old road grade.
69.29	111.58	Note the gargantuan rhododendron bushes up the slope to the left.
69.39	111.74	The QT is now alongside Saunders Run. This beautiful hollow was severely damaged during the infamous tornadoes of 1985. A major relocation of the QT was sent up the hillside to the right and onto a series of jeep roads all the way to Parker Dam State Park. It was not until 2001 when the QT was restored to its former route in Saunders Hollow, after the forest had finally recovered. [Seeley, 31] As you proceed up this hollow on the QT, there are many possible campsites on both sides of the creek.
69.46	111.85	Turn right and cross a footbridge over Saunders Run, which offers good water quality all the way upstream. Do not confuse this creek with Sanders Draft, which the QT walked alongside about 22 miles ago. After the bridge, the trail heads slightly uphill and diverges from the creek for a while.
69.54	111.98	Cross a usually dry run then pass a junction with the Fairview Trail on the right. (That trail leads to a vista over Saunders Hollow and an elk viewing area that was constructed in 2025. It then continues southwest along various old roads to the state park.)
69.67	112.18	After briefly reuniting with Saunders Run, climb up the embankment to get around a tight spot in the hollow. You soon return to the creekside and proceed through a nice camping area. Ahead, the trail has a hard time staying level, and you rise above the creek several times, then come back down. There are many nice camping areas along the stream all the way up the hollow, though some will require a scramble from the trail.

MI	KM	DESCRIPTION
69.84	112.47	Cross a murky side channel of the run and continue on bottomland surrounded by intertwining rivulets.
69.94	112.63	Turn left then right during another climb partway up the side of the hollow. The trail levels off and remains about 30 to 50 feet above the creek for a while.
70.23	113.09	Cross a usually dry tributary then climb up the embankment again.
70.32	113.24	Still about 50 feet above Saunders Run, note the multiple channels and island below you to the left. That is another nice camping area if you choose to scramble down there.
70.44	113.43	Turn left and descend to the creekside.
70.58	113.65	Watch blazes carefully at a spot where an overgrown old haul road plunges down the side of the canyon. The QT bears left and descends.
70.61	113.71	Hop across some muddy side channels in a fairly soggy bottomland area.
70.67	113.80	Bear right for another brief climb away from the run.
70.75	113.93	Turn abruptly right, away from Saunders Run, and head up a trail segment that goes around an environmentally sensitive area.
71.09	114.47	The trail is now following a solid old railroad grade slightly above the run.
71.28	114.78	With giant boulders all around, some of which are on top of Saunders Run, turn abruptly right at a post sign and climb ruggedly. Here the QT has been detoured around another environmentally sensitive spot.
71.44	115.04	Bear right at the junction with the north end of the Cut Off Trail, which heads left back down to Saunders Run, then leads to the southern segment of the QT at its 3.47 mi point. After the junction, the QT continues a moderate climb out of Saunders Hollow.

MI	KM	DESCRIPTION
71.56	115.23	The trail levels off near a dry campsite and curves left.
71.82	115.65	Cross an old logging road and continue ahead, easily across the flat top of the plateau.
71.90	115.78	Trail register; please sign in.
71.99	115.93	Cross Tyler Road; parking at this crossing is not recommended. This is the second time the QT crosses Tyler Road.
72.08	116.07	Watch the blazes carefully as the trail makes a few surprise turns. A hunting camp becomes visible to the right.
72.21	116.28	Turn right at a junction with the Spurline Trail. (That trail heads across a footbridge and leads easily to the southern segment of the QT at its 1.30 mi point.) The QT is now on an old railroad grade alongside an unnamed tributary of Laurel Run; acceptable water quality.
72.25	116.34	Cross a pipeline swath with some muddy spots and a partially useful old snowmobile bridge, then bear left.
72.39	116.57	Cross the run and continue ahead on the old grade, descending gently.
72.45	116.67	Bear left for a brief climb up a minor ridgeline. The meadows in this area offer some possibilities for camping.
72.64	116.97	Cross an intermittent stream; not suitable for drinking.
72.72	117.10	Cross a powerline swath. In this area you cross the border into Parker Dam State Park, so no primitive camping is permitted for the remainder of the Quehanna Trail.
72.77	117.18	Cross a muddy run; not suitable for drinking. The trail next curves broadly to the right (west).
73.04	117.62	Just before a grassy field that is visible ahead (a state park maintenance area), turn sharply right.

MI	KM	DESCRIPTION
73.13	117.76	Turn left onto the gravel Fairview Road. The post sign at the turn says that you are on the Quehanna Trail, Spurline Trail, and Fairview Trail. The QT heads southwest toward Parker Dam State Park.
73.22	117.91	Continue straight ahead at a road junction.
73.34	118.10	A footpath on the left leads to the state park campground; continue straight ahead on the dirt road.
73.47	118.31	A yellow-blazed state park trail diverges to the right. The QT continues straight ahead, and the road underfoot becomes paved. Walk around a vehicle gate, then past an RV dump station and a couple of drinking water taps. The official Parker Dam State Park campground, with restrooms, is on the left, and the dam and artificial lake are on the right.
73.60	118.52	Continue straight ahead on the paved road, past another campground driveway and a speed limit sign.
73.73	118.73	Reach the end of the Quehanna Trail loop at the official trailhead and parking area on Fairview Road. Here, the loop begins again by going up the wide path to the left.

GUIDE TO THE CUT OFF TRAIL

This short and scenic trail is traditionally used to form a great loop hike that connects two ends of the Quehanna Trail. That loop is 7.44 miles long and can be started at Parker Dam State Park (see the "Logistics of the Quehanna Trail Network" chapter earlier in this book). The southern end of the Cutoff Trail is also just 0.18 mi (0.29 km) east of the QT's parking lot on Tyler Road. This guide describes the Cutoff Trail in the northbound direction.

MI	KM	DESCRIPTION
0.00	0.00	From the 3.47 mi point on the southern segment of the Quehanna Trail, the yellow-blazed Cut Off Trail heads to the north through a flat area. Note that a few of the trail's former blue blazes are still visible but can be disregarded.
0.17	0.27	Pass through an area of dense young beech trees, with a few older trees of other species standing guard above.
0.28	0.45	Turn left and begin a mild descent. The Cut Off Trail remains uneventful for about the next half mile, but it is quite curvy, so watch the blazes carefully.
0.41	0.66	Pass through a small meadow that might serve as an unconventional camping spot.
0.74	1.19	Turn sharply right in a rocky area and head toward Saunders Hollow.
0.81	1.30	Turn sharply right twice and begin a steep descent down a ridgeline. Watch the blazes carefully.
0.84	1.35	Switchback sharply to the left. Note the large boulders below.

MI	KM	DESCRIPTION
0.91	1.47	The trail crosses an upper tributary of Saunders Run (good water quality) and turns right, roughly paralleling the run downstream.
1.16	1.87	Bear slightly to the left across a wide pipeline swath. Note the extensive tire tread damage from off-road vehicles.
1.34	2.16	Descend through an area of large, moss-covered boulders. Saunders Run is now to the right.
1.41	2.27	You are now alongside Saunders Run (good water quality) in a very scenic hollow. There are some possible campsites on both sides of the stream.
1.45	2.33	Cross a small tributary stream (acceptable water quality in season) then turn right. Continue following Saunders Run downstream.
1.58	2.54	Pass alongside a series of small waterfalls in Saunders Run, caused by plentiful boulders.

Saunders Run alongside the Cut Off Trail.

MI	KM	DESCRIPTION
1.62	2.61	Turn sharply left twice and climb steeply away from Saunders Run.
1.68	2.71	Turn right, then reach the north end of the Cut Off Trail at a large boulder on the northern segment of the Quehanna Trail, at its 71.44 mi point. Turn left to follow the QT westbound, or right for eastbound.

GUIDE TO THE WEST CROSS CONNECTOR TRAIL

The West Cross Connector Trail is often used to form a loop hike with the western segments of the Quehanna Trail. That loop is 19.81 miles long and can be started at Parker Dam State Park (see the "Logistics of the Quehanna Trail Network" chapter earlier in this book). The West Cross Connector should also be hiked in its own right; its biggest highlight is Medix Run Vista. This guide describes the West Cross Connector Trail in the northbound direction.

MI	KM	DESCRIPTION
0.00	0.00	The Quehanna Trail West Cross Connector (QTWCC) departs from the main Quehanna Trail at the crossing of Wallace Mines Road, at the 4.95 mi point on the QT. The yellow-blazed QTWCC heads northeast on Wallace Mines Road, on which the blazes are very sparse and are only on telephone poles. Confusingly, this road is also known on some maps as simply Wallace Mine Road. Follow the road easily for the next 0.76 mi (1.22 km). Around the first curve in the road, note the large wetland to the left. There are some parking spots at wide areas along the road.
0.09	0.14	"Three R Rd." (a hunting camp driveway) on the right.
0.25	0.40	Pass another hunting camp driveway on the left.
0.76	1.22	Just after a double blaze on a telephone pole, turn left off Wallace Mines Road and onto an old woods lane.
0.81	1.30	Stay on the old road as it curves left.
0.86	1.38	Bear right through what appears to be an old vehicle turnaround.

MI	KM	DESCRIPTION
1.20	1.93	Cross another heavily overgrown old road. Continue ahead.
1.29	2.08	Begin a mild descent into a small hollow with many hemlocks.
1.49	2.40	After exiting the dark gulch, bear left, still on the same old woods road.
1.81	2.91	Turn right then left through a muddy area.
1.89	3.04	As another old woods road appears to your right, cross Caledonia Pike and continue straight ahead on a narrower footpath. There are one or two possible parking spots in wide areas along the road. Ahead, note that the West Cross Connector temporarily shares its path with another trail called the Shaggers Inn Loop.
1.98	3.19	Watch the blazes carefully through a dark stand of hemlocks.
2.21	3.56	Note the very large meadow to the left with a lake in the distance. This is the Shaggers Inn impoundment, which was built in a wetland area in the late 1980s as a stop for migrating waterfowl. Shaggers Inn was apparently a tavern in the former town of Huntley near here. [Seeley, 33] Next, the QTWCC makes a broad curve to the right (east).
2.33	3.75	Make an abrupt left turn at a double blaze. Watch the blazes carefully in this area.
2.40	3.86	Turn left and cross an intermittent run (poor water quality).
2.50	4.03	Turn right and cross an upper tributary of Trout Run (acceptable water quality).
2.56	4.12	Turn left twice in a small clearing. The QTWCC soon enters a very large meadow.
2.74	4.41	Exit the meadow into a forest that features a few ancient trees standing above many more, younger, ones.

One of several meadows traversed by the West Cross Connector Trail.

MI	KM	DESCRIPTION
2.76	4.44	Pass through another meadow, much smaller than the last.
2.83	4.56	Hop over a small run; not suitable for drinking.
3.22	5.19	Cross Shaggers Inn Road and a small parking lot. Continue straight ahead and walk around a vehicle gate to join a recently active logging road. The QTWCC follows this road for the next 1.36 mi (2.19 km). The road soon starts to descend.
3.33	5.36	Pass a former vista to the right (east) that is now overgrown; the view is much better when the leaves are down. You can see the flat plateau landscape as far as the Renovo area on a clear day, with some ridges and canyons in the distance. Continue on the logging road uneventfully.
4.19	6.75	Cross a wide pipeline swath and continue straight ahead, still on the same logging road. There is a partial vista to the right into a branch of Medix Hollow. The road next descends and makes a broad curve to the left (west) into a different branch of the hollow.

MI	KM	DESCRIPTION
4.50	7.25	The logging road makes a broad curve to the right (north).
4.58	7.38	Watch carefully for a double blaze, where you bear right off the logging road and onto an old grassy lane that heads toward a field.
4.74	7.63	Cross the field, which covers an old drilling station, and walk to the left of the rusted vent pipe. Watch for the next blaze at the back of the field and continue into the woods on a narrow footpath through a rocky area.
4.92	7.92	Turn left twice amidst large boulders. You are now above yet another branch of Medix Hollow.
5.08	8.18	Watch the blazes carefully for some surprise turns during a brief climb.
5.17	8.33	Pass through a patch of giant rhododendron that forces several curves into the trail.
5.56	8.95	Pass through an outcropping of boulders and begin a very steep descent. This is the beginning of a particularly brutal plunge down the steepest grade in the Quehanna Trail network. The QTWCC dives more than 750 feet in just the next half mile.
5.72	9.21	After a nice (but dry and windy) camping spot, resume the very steep descent amidst boulders. Medix Run Vista opens up ahead of you. This is one of the premier vistas in the entire Quehanna Trail network. You can see down into multiple branches of the hollow to the north, parts of Sinnemahoning Creek's valley near the village of Medix Run, and the hills and plateau beyond. Note that this vista tends to get overgrown and must be periodically cleared out by forestry personnel. Try not to be distracted by the view and watch your footing during the treacherous descent.
5.79	9.32	At the lower edge of the vista area, turn sharply left and begin a difficult series of switchbacks.

The top of Medix Run Vista; a nice spot to tighten your
bootlaces for some fancy footwork.

MI	KM	DESCRIPTION
(cont.)		One reason why the QTWCC is traditionally described northbound is because very little climbing is required to reach Medix Run Vista in this direction. You will soon find that approaching this vista in the southbound direction would be ridiculously more difficult. It was quite harsh for the trail builders too. [Seeley, 34]
5.81	9.36	Switchback left, then right, down an incredibly steep grade. Use extreme caution during wet or icy conditions, and also in the autumn when there are loose, freshly fallen leaves on the ground.
5.85	9.42	Switchback left, then right again, still extremely steep downhill.

MI	KM	DESCRIPTION
5.88	9.47	Yet another multiple switchback; watch blazes carefully. Here the trail has been carefully routed to prevent erosion, so resist the temptation to take shortcuts through the switchbacks. The trail eventually curves to the right (southeast) onto a brief sidehill segment.
5.93	9.55	Turn sharply left and resume the brutal descent. Medix Grade Road is visible below.
6.01	9.68	The trail has leveled off temporarily on sidehill above a small hunting camp that sits at the corner of Medix Grade Road and Little Medix Road.
6.04	9.73	Turn right and resume the very steep descent yet again. (Almost done!)
6.10	9.82	Turn sharply left onto an old road grade above Little Medix Road. The trail briefly detours around what appears to be a small landslide, then rejoins the grade at an old gas well site. The road grade next descends moderately toward Little Medix Road.
6.27	10.10	Bottom out on Little Media Road at the end of the West Cross Connector Trail. The main Quehanna Trail follows the road in this area; westbound is left and eastbound is right. You are at the 65.14 mi point on the QT.

GUIDE TO THE EAST CROSS CONNECTOR TRAIL

The East Cross Connector Trail is often used to form a backpacking loop of 3-4 days with the eastern segments of the Quehanna Trail. That loop is 40.81 miles long (see the "Logistics of the Quehanna Trail Network" chapter earlier in this book.) The East Cross Connector should also be hiked in its own right; it passes through many particularly scenic meadows and abounds in pleasant camping spots. It also leads to several short spur trails in Quehanna Wild Area that offer dozens of options for creative loop hikes. This guide describes the East Cross Connector Trail in the southbound direction. Note that the northern end cannot be reached by car; the available access points are described below.

MI	KM	DESCRIPTION
0.00	0.00	The yellow-blazed Quehanna Trail East Cross Connector (QTECC) departs southbound down the one-lane Losey Road from the 51.70 mi point on the main Quehanna Trail. This northern end of the QTECC cannot be reached by car because the road is gated about three-quarters of a mile south of here.
0.29	0.47	Stay on the road past a junction with the CC Ski Trail, also yellow-blazed, which goes to the right.
0.44	0.71	At a post sign, turn left off the dirt road and onto a footpath.
0.75	1.21	Turn left at a double blaze in a generally nondescript area.
1.20	1.93	Turn right at a double blaze, with a small meadow visible to the left.
1.27	2.05	Pass through another small meadow.

MI	KM	DESCRIPTION
1.35	2.17	Cross a log bridge over Roaring Run (it is much more "roaring" elsewhere in its course). Questionable water quality. There are some nice camping spots in this area.
1.37	2.21	Continue straight ahead at a junction with the Teaberry Trail (also yellow-blazed). NOTE: There are many trail signs ahead, at the junctions with other yellow-blazed trails. These junctions can be confusing so be sure to follow the acronym "QTECC" for Quehanna Trail East Cross Connector.
1.75	2.82	Continue straight ahead at a junction with the Marion Brooks Natural Area Loop Trail (also yellow-blazed). The QTECC makes up one side of this very scenic loop, which is approximately four miles around. The loop skirts the edge of, but does not enter, its namesake natural area due to state restrictions on trails in environmentally sensitive places.
1.84	2.96	Enter a large meadow.
1.86	3.00	Continue straight ahead at a junction with the Lincoln Loop ski trail (also yellow-blazed).
1.97	3.17	Cross a skier's bridge over Paige Run. Acceptable water quality.
2.00	3.22	A short and barely visible side trail on the left leads to the ruins of an old cabin.
2.17	3.49	Pass another side trail that goes to a small parking lot on the left, then cross Quehanna Highway and continue straight ahead into a pine plantation. (Be careful; speed limit is 55 mph). Trail signs that have stood at this crossing have been repeatedly knocked over by vehicles—apparently a local drunken pastime. Recent signposts were reinforced by a hidden iron bar and anchored in hundreds of pounds of concrete. If any miscreants have attempted to drive over these, their vehicles probably suffered far more damage. [Seeley, 35]

MI	KM	DESCRIPTION
2.28	3.67	Continue straight ahead at the second junction with the Lincoln Loop ski trail (also yellow-blazed). The parking lot for the Beaver Run Wildlife Viewing area, just off Quehanna Highway, can be reached by following that trail to the left.
2.68	4.32	Turn right through a soggy hemlock grove.
2.81	4.52	Reach a trail register; please sign in. The QTECC turns left onto an old road grade. (The southern segment of the Marion Brooks Natural Area Loop Trail, also yellow-blazed, heads right on the road grade.)
2.86	4.61	Bear right off the road grade and onto trail.
3.06	4.93	Enter a system of expansive meadows. A large artificial lake called the Beaver Run Shallow Water Impoundment becomes visible in the far distance to the left.
3.35	5.39	Bear left away from the meadow and into the trees, then turn left again.

The Beaver Run Shallow Water Impoundment: a clunky name
for a scenic manmade lake.

MI	KM	DESCRIPTION
3.48	5.60	Bear right onto another old road grade. The Beaver Run impoundment is visible again to the left.
3.59	5.78	Bear right off the road grade and onto trail again.
3.73	6.01	At a nice camping area near the lakeshore, turn right onto another segment of the old road grade. This artificial lake was built in 1979 by damming a generally soggy wetland area. The lake has become a crucial stop for migrating waterfowl, and other wildlife appear to enjoy the area. Note the dead trees sticking out of the water, which are now being used for duck boxes. [Seeley, 37] Elk, bald eagles, and golden eagles have been reported in this area. I once saw a bald eagle sitting in one of the lake's dead trees, and an enormous aerie (eagle's nest) nearby included someone's T-shirt as building material. I wonder if the person was still wearing it when the eagle decided to take it.
3.86	6.22	Turn left briefly onto the low earthen dam, then immediately turn right at a post sign. You soon rejoin the road grade.
3.92	6.31	Turn right onto a recently active gravel logging road. (To the left, this road is initially parallel to the dam, then continues about half a mile to the parking lot for the Beaver Run Wildlife Viewing area.)
4.01	6.46	Cross a pipeline swath.
4.13	6.65	Cross a powerline swath, where the gravel ends (at the time of writing). Continue ahead on an old grassy lane through meadows. Watch blazes carefully.
4.35	7.00	Pass through a large meadow, parallel to the powerline. This is one of many meadows in the area that are being used as feed plots for elk.
4.63	7.46	Turn left off the grassy lane and onto trail. Descend gently into another meadow along Beaver Run. A little later, curve right alongside a large beaver-built pond.

MI	KM	DESCRIPTION
4.80	7.73	Turn left and cross the long bridge over the pond. This bridge was built by Keystone Trails Association and state forest personnel in 2024, and is the latest of several bridges to cross Beaver Run and/or one of its ponds. You will soon see that several previous bridges were knocked aside by all manner of natural calamities.

After the bridge, turn right, climb briefly, and continue southbound slightly above the bottom of the valley. The trail remains parallel to this very scenic and open valley, which was created by generations of beaver dams. The ponds created by the dams killed trees and then gradually filled with silt, resulting in relatively soggy flat areas where new trees are unlikely to grow. The ultimate result is a flat, treeless valley.

This particular area was also ravaged by the infamous tornadoes of 1985 and a forest fire in 1988. [Seeley, 37–39] Meanwhile the occasional heavy thunderstorm can wipe out a beaver dam, after which the critters rebuild somewhere nearby, resulting in constant reshuffling of the landscape.

A beaver lodge in a beaver pond on Beaver Run.
Yes, there are many beavers in this area.

MI	KM	DESCRIPTION
4.98	8.02	Note the discarded old footbridges visible below. These were on a former route of the QTECC, which was abandoned in 2000 when beavers dammed the run and wrecked the bridges. Trail maintainers built a long boardwalk over the newly wet area, only for that human construction project to be destroyed by a hurricane in 2004. [Seeley, 37-38] The beavers' dam has since been washed away by stormy weather, after which their former pond mostly silted up. Next, the trail briefly returns to the bottom of the valley before curving broadly to the left (southeast) into another system of meadows.
5.14	8.28	Hop over a small run (not suitable for drinking) then turn left, upstream. Next, the QTECC curves gradually to the right and heads toward higher ground. Watch carefully for faraway blazes.
5.47	8.81	Continue ahead at a junction with the Bridge Trail (also yellow-blazed) which goes to the right.
5.75	9.26	Turn left at a double blaze; the QTECC is now back in the forest.
6.10	9.82	Continue ahead at a junction with the Meeker Trail (also yellow-blazed) which goes to the right. The directional arrows on the signpost here could cause confusion.
6.60	10.63	Cross the corner of another large meadow, then turn right onto an old railroad grade alongside Meeker Run. Acceptable water quality, though it would be wise to go downstream a bit.
6.68	10.76	Continue ahead at a junction with the Ralph Seeley Trail (also yellow-blazed) which goes to the left. A legendary Pennsylvania trail builder, Seeley built dozens of miles of hiking and skiing trails in Quehanna Wild Area and was the impetus behind the long-distance Allegheny Front Trail in Centre County.
6.96	11.21	Nice camping spots can be found on both sides of the stream.

MI	KM	DESCRIPTION
7.02	11.30	Reach a potentially confusing staggered four-way intersection with the Meeker Trail (also yellow-blazed). The QTECC bears left, then right, and continues southbound parallel to Meeker Run. There is more nice camping in this area; note the mysterious building stone on the right at the junction.
7.19	11.58	Hop across a small run; not suitable for drinking. It appears that there was once a railroad bridge here.
7.27	11.71	Pass a nice waterfall and skinny-dipping spot in Meeker Run to the left.
7.31	11.77	Turn right and pass through a formation of large boulders. The trail becomes rocky for a while.
7.45	12.00	Continue ahead at a junction with the Crawford Vista Trail (also yellow-blazed) which climbs the hill to the right and reaches a vista in about nine-tenths of a mile.
7.62	12.27	After a rough but brief descent, you are now alongside Meeker Run again, in a pretty area where boulders create several riffles and waterfalls.
7.68	12.37	After crossing a muddy side channel (not suitable for drinking), cross Meeker Run on an old bridge. The structure to the right is the remains of a pump house associated with the old nuclear reactor up on Reactor Road. [Seeley, 40; see also Appendix B later in this book.] Slightly downstream from here, radioactive waste from the reactor was dumped into Meeker Run in the late 1950s.
7.71	12.42	Cross a small side stream (questionable water quality) then turn left for a steep but brief climb.
7.77	12.51	The trail levels off on an old road grade that is probably an ancient version of Lost Run Road.
7.83	12.61	Turn right on Lost Run Road and head downhill. Stay on this road for the next 0.63 mi (1.01 km). You soon cross the boundary into State Game Lands #34; no camping is allowed for the remainder of the QTECC.

MI	KM	DESCRIPTION
8.27	13.32	Mosquito Creek comes into view at the site of an old splash dam. [Seeley, 41]
8.33	13.41	Cross the road bridge over Mosquito Creek and pass a parking spot.
8.46	13.62	As the road curves sharply to the right, turn left into a small grassy area and re-enter the woods. The QTECC scrambles down a steep embankment. Next, after leveling off briefly, the trail begins a tough sidehill segment above Mosquito Creek, which is sometimes visible down to the left.
8.73	14.06	Turn right and climb steeply to a higher bench on the hillside. The entire QTECC has been very easy until this point, but it suddenly becomes very difficult for its final six-tenths of a mile.
8.81	14.19	Reach a rapidly plunging stream (acceptable water quality in season) and resume a very steep climb out of the gorge.
8.91	14.35	Pass a spring that forms the run (not suitable for drinking up here). Get ready for one more steep blast out of the gorge, after which the climb becomes more moderate though there is still a long way to go.
9.19	14.80	The trail curves left, parallel to Lost Run Road. Watch blazes carefully.
9.22	14.85	Reach Lost Run Road again and turn left. Stay on this road for the remainder of the QTECC—0.13 mi (0.21 km).
9.35	15.06	Southern end of the QTECC, at the 20.24 mi point on the Quehanna Trail. The QT crosses Lost Run Road here; eastbound is to the left and westbound is to the right. There is a small parking lot a bit further up the road.

GUIDE TO THE OLD SINNEMAHONING TRAIL

The Old Sinnemahoning Trail (OST) follows a mysterious old road from the village of Wyside along Sinnemahoning Creek to Three Runs Road high above on the plateau, intersecting with the northeastern segment of the Quehanna Trail along the way. The OST is a crucial link from the QT to another long-distance backpacking resource: the Donut Hole Trail. (See the "Logistics of the Quehanna Trail Network" chapter earlier in this book for details.)

From Wyside, the OST follows the old road steeply uphill for more than an entire mile. I have hiked thousands of miles in Pennsylvania, and this is the one of the most extensive climbs on a hiking trail that I have experienced in the state. The elevation gain from absolute bottom to absolute top (about halfway to Three Runs Road) is about 1300 feet. Then at the top of the climb the old road suddenly becomes almost entirely flat on top of the Quehanna plateau. After this point the OST is uneventful for the hiker, but it suddenly makes sense as a transportation route.

The exact purpose of this old road is unclear, though I have learned from hiking historian Ralph Seeley and longtime forester Wally Finn that the road was most likely used in the late 1800s by workers in the Sinnemahoning area to commute by horseback to faraway jobs in Karthaus.

As a hiking trail, the OST currently ends at Three Runs Road. However, there is evidence that the workers' road continued west on that road, headed south on what is now an equestrian trail called Moyer Run Loop (but still labelled as the OST on some maps), turned east on what is now Reservoir Road, then continued south, roughly parallel to the modern Quehanna Highway and PA 879 all the way to the West Branch Susquehanna River at Karthaus.

MI	KM	DESCRIPTION
0.00	0.00	The yellow-blazed Old Sinnemahoning Trail (OST) starts at the corner of Jerry Run Road and Hardinger Street in Wyside, on the east side of the road bridge over Wykoff Run. The OST heads southwest, uphill, on an old woods road. Stick to this track because the surrounding land around the bottom of the trail is private. Be prepared, because you are about to embark on a relentless climb for the next 1.12 mi (1.80 km), with an elevation gain of more than one thousand feet in that short distance. This is one of the steepest and longest climbs on a hiking trail in all of Pennsylvania. Since the beginning of the OST is surrounded by private land, no primitive camping is allowed for about the first third of a mile, though you are unlikely to find a good spot for it anyway.
0.05	0.08	Bear left at a fork in the jeep road and climb more steeply. This is the strenuous state of affairs until the top of the mountain.
1.01	1.63	Finally, some good news—when the leaves are down, you can now see over the top of the mountain to the right. That means that you are somewhere near the top of this one.
1.12	1.80	The trail finally begins to level off on top of the plateau. The old road grade becomes narrower thanks to shrubbery and young trees. Watch blazes carefully as the trail makes some surprise curves in this area.
1.45	2.33	The OST is now rising moderately again, to get around a small knob on top of the plateau.
1.59	2.56	The trail flattens out again, curving broadly to the left and trending away from Wykoff Hollow. From here, most of the rest of the OST is level and easy. Ahead, the old road occasionally narrows to a footpath through fields of ferns and mountain laurel.
1.93	3.11	Pass through a jungle of giant rhododendron with some mountain laurel and young hemlocks mixed in.

This old road, now known as the OST, offers an
easygoing hike after you get to the top of the mountain.

MI	KM	DESCRIPTION
2.78	4.48	Enter an area featuring several vernal pools in the springtime. These are crucial breeding spots for amphibians.
3.70	5.96	The OST climbs briefly up a minor ridgeline.
4.05	6.52	Cross an overgrown pipeline swath, with an old valve apparatus on the right. The OST's road grade becomes considerably wider.
4.34	6.99	Reach the first junction with the Quehanna Trail, at that trail's 39.86 mi point. The QT comes in from the right, having just climbed out of Upper Pine Hollow, and turns onto the OST. Straight ahead, the two trails are concurrent for the next 0.24 mi (0.39 km). Note that a sign at the junction lists a distance to

MI	KM	DESCRIPTION
(cont.)		"Three Runs" via the OST, but this refers to the creek of that name which is farther away than Three Runs Road at the current end of the OST
4.58	7.38	At a four-way junction of grassy lanes, the Quehanna Trail turns left. The Old Sinnemahoning Trail continues straight ahead, still on the same woods road. Blazes become less frequent. Note the extensive fields to the right, which are being managed to attract elk. This area also features extensive vernal pools in the spring.
4.74	7.63	Continue straight ahead across a wide powerline swath. Stay on the same woods lane, with very little excitement, for the next 1.98 mi (3.19 km).
6.72	10.82	Walk around a vehicle gate and head toward the dirt road ahead.
6.77	10.90	End of the modern, yellow-blazed Old Sinnemahoning Trail at Three Runs Road. This is a possible parking spot. The Quehanna Trail crosses this road at a state forestry parking lot about one mile to the northeast. Also, across the road, the yellow-blazed #15 Trail departs to the east and leads about one mile to the QT near Lower Three Runs Run.

GUIDE TO THE BEAR RUN TRAIL

The Bear Run Trail connects two points on the northwestern segment of the Quehanna Trail, and it is in fact a former route of the QT that was rechristened as a new trail when the QT was rerouted to the south in 2016. The reason for the rerouting of the main trail was a series of failed footbridges over Medix Run, the last of which was never replaced. The creek must now be crossed by hikers on the Bear Run Trail, and without a bridge. This crossing must not be attempted during high water periods. (For more details, see "Appendix C: Medix Run and the Bear Run Trail.")

Do not discount the Bear Run Trail just because it is now an "alternate" route for something else. Notwithstanding the wet creek crossing, it offers a pleasant hiking experience with its own scenic features, including a vista and a series of bucolic meadows and wetlands along Laurel Run.

MI	KM	DESCRIPTION
0.00	0.00	The yellow-blazed Bear Run Trail begins at the 63.64 mi point on the Quehanna Trail in Medix Hollow, at the sign warning of a water crossing ahead at Medix Run. Begin by heading west and descending toward the bottom of the canyon. NOTE: The phrase "Shallow Water Crossing" on the sign means that you should attempt to do so only when the water is shallow during dry periods.
0.05	0.08	Turn right at a large double-trunked tree and head more steeply downhill toward Medix Grade Road.
0.08	0.13	Watch blazes carefully through a couple of curves then scramble down an embankment to Medix Grade Road. Continue straight ahead down a driveway to a pair of reservable car campsites. (Do not park in this area.)

MI	KM	DESCRIPTION
0.11	0.17	Within the camping area, turn left into a reservable spot at another sign warning of the creek crossing. Follow a footpath beyond a small car-blocking boulder.
0.13	0.21	Watch for a double blaze at a spot where you can see the next single blaze on the other side of Medix Run. Turn right and cross the run somewhere in this area as best you can. During dry periods it may be viable to hop across the creek on rocks while staying dry. At other times you may have to wade across knee-deep water. During wet periods the crossing may be completely unviable and even dangerous. Remember that this stream has knocked out multiple footbridges on the old route of the Quehanna Trail, with the most recent mishap occurring a few hundred yards downstream from this spot in 2014.
0.15	0.24	After crossing the creek, locate the next yellow blaze and continue into the woods. Hop over an old rock wall and pass yet another sign about the creek crossing—this one facing the other way. Next, turn right.
0.19	0.31	Turn left and scramble up an embankment, then head into Bear Hollow, parallel to the run of the same name. Bear Run is intermittent for some of the year, though the water quality is acceptable when it is flowing.
0.27	0.43	Pass some waterfalls in Bear Run. There are some slim possibilities for camping in this area.
0.33	0.53	Cross Bear Run on rocks. Continue climbing up the hollow for the next 0.71 mi (1.14 km). As is typical of hollows in this region, the climb gets steeper and rockier as you go up. Also, since this is a former route of the Quehanna Trail, you may see some old orange blazes that can be helpful; but watch for the newer yellow blazes for the modern Bear Run Trail.
1.04	1.67	Near the top of the hollow, turn right, cross what is left of the watercourse, and head up the ridgeline on the far side.

MI	KM	DESCRIPTION
1.15	1.85	After the trail finally levels off on top of the plateau, turn sharply left away from Bear Hollow.
1.54	2.48	Begin a descent into a shallow hollow.
1.78	2.87	Cross Caledonia Pike then bear right. Watch blazes carefully. There is no convenient parking at this crossing, but there are some artificially cleared logging areas a few hundred yards to the left (south) that might serve as parking spots.
1.99	3.20	Cross an unnamed run (questionable water quality) and scramble up an embankment.
2.29	3.69	Bear right at a dry, open-air campsite. Here you will find a vista to the west, down a hollow toward Laurel Run. On a clear day you can see mountaintops on the far side of Weedville and Penfield.
2.45	3.95	Turn left and descend into a side hollow.
2.49	4.01	Cross the unnamed run that flows down the side hollow (acceptable water quality when flowing).
2.59	4.17	After veering inland a bit, bear right alongside the run again.
2.69	4.33	Cross the hollow's main run on rocks (acceptable water quality when flowing). Turn right and then bear left away from the stream.
2.72	4.38	Bear right onto an old forest road. A short distance ahead, note the small landslide below the road.
3.26	5.25	The old road is now at the bottom of the hollow. This is a nice camping area but note that there are some hunting camps nearby.
3.33	5.36	Turn left onto another old road grade. (Straight ahead, you can see a hunting camp driveway with vehicle bridge.)

MI	KM	DESCRIPTION
3.36	5.41	Cross a wide wet spot formed by several seep springs flowing toward Laurel Run. Next you will pass several murky pools that are breeding spots for amphibians. (None of these are suitable for drinking.) Continue ahead on the old road.
3.72	5.99	The old road rises above a sparsely forested wetland with Laurel Run in the distance.
4.11	6.62	Near the top of a long, drawn-out climb, pass a boulder vehicle barrier.
4.15	6.68	The old road curves to the left and begins to descend.
4.50	7.25	Cross a small run at the top of a waterfall. The wide Laurel Run is now just to your right. Next, the old road grade begins to rise for a while before descending again.
5.05	8.13	Walk around a vehicle gate.
5.11	8.23	Turn left on Saunders Road. (To the right, near the road bridge over Laurel Run, there is an old car campsite where a few vehicles can park.) The rest of the Bear Run Trail is on this road.
5.27	8.49	Saunders Road goes through a hairpin curve. In approximately the middle of the curve, note the small footbridge on the left where the orange-blazed Quehanna Trail emerges from a side hollow. The run that meets Saunders Road here is a good water source. This is the end of the Bear Run Trail, at the 68.25 mi point on the QT. The QT continues straight ahead, southbound, on Saunders Road.

APPENDIX A:
MOSQUITO CREEK AND CORPORATION DAM

Starting at about the 24.24 mi point as described in this guide, the Quehanna Trail walks across a flat bottomland before reaching the wide and rapid Mosquito Creek, where a series of footbridges have failed. This deceptively normal landscape is actually the scene of enormous environmental damage, dating back to the 1870s and continuing to have effects to this day. The story begins with a splash dam.

SPLASH DAMS

During the Pennsylvania logging era of the late 1800s, loggers fanned out into the forests to find valuable trees, conducting operations far from roads, railroads, and navigable rivers. This led to a problem with getting the felled logs out of the hollows and down off the mountaintops. Natural streams were the answer, and engineers came up with a temporary structure called a splash dam.

A typically earthen dam would be built across a stream, with a wooden gate in the middle that could be opened and closed. Loggers would place recently felled trees in the small artificial lake that formed behind the dam. When all was ready, the wooden gate would be opened and the lake water would surge forth and head downstream, carrying all the logs with it. When that shipment of logs had gone on its way, the gate in the dam would be closed and the process would start again. Some longer streams had several of these contraptions along their lengths, and eventually the logs would be transported to their ultimate destination faraway downstream, usually a sawmill or rail depot.

This was a clumsy and labor-intensive transport method until nimble narrow-gauge railroads became more prevalent in the region. (Many

Pennsylvania hiking trails follow these old railroad grades, especially in rugged hollows.) Loggers surely welcomed the railroads whole-heartedly. According to Pennsylvania hiking authority and historian Tom Thwaites, when a splash dam was opened, some loggers were tasked with running alongside the torrent and pushing beached logs back into the water before it subsided. This line of work apparently resulted in a lot of deaths. Mercifully, a guy would be crushed to death by rampaging logs long before he had the time to drown.

These splash dams were usually small affairs on narrow streams that flowed rapidly down steep-sided hollows. Due to the spread of narrow-gauge railroads, splash dams became obsolete by around 1885. Since then, most have disappeared without a trace, but a well-preserved specimen can still be seen at Eddy Lick Run in northern Centre County, along the Chuck Keiper Trail.

CORPORATION DAM

Near the Quehanna Trail's crossing of Mosquito Creek, there was once an unusually long splash dam called Corporation Dam. There were at least nine splash dams in the Mosquito Creek watershed, which the loggers probably used in a coordinated fashion. Corporation Dam was one of the largest known splash dams in the region—a couple of hundred yards long, at least ten feet tall, and mostly made of compacted soil. Its artificial lake was also unusually large, probably about half a mile long and up to a quarter of a mile across at some points in the unusually wide valley of Mosquito Creek. Though it is now long gone (a couple of overgrown earthen embankments are all that remain), Corporation Dam remains a noteworthy historical artifact from beyond the metaphorical grave.

According to archival research performed by Ralph Seeley, Corporation Dam was built in approximately 1870 and was only in operation for a few years, until the surrounding watershed was completely denuded of trees and the loggers lost interest. [For additional historical information, see Seeley, 14–15.] Despite this short period of operation, the environmental damage was immense, proving that degradation can continue for decades and even centuries after short-lived industrial ventures move on.

The current landscape along Mosquito Creek is considerably higher than it was before Corporation Dam was built. The ground traversed by the Quehanna Trail was once at the bottom of the dam's large artificial lake. When the dam was in operation, Mosquito Creek, Gifford Run, and Twelve Mile Run all flowed into the lake, and during the logging era these streams carried considerable amounts of mud from the denuded hillsides where trees had been removed and soil was easily washed away. When the water flow suddenly slowed down at the lake, the mud was dumped at the bottom, forming a flat layer at least eight feet thick in places.

When the loggers abandoned the splash dam after just a few years, they probably just left its gate open and drained the lake. Mosquito Creek then endeavored to regain something like its natural course, first wearing away the wooden gate and then most of the earthen ramparts as well. Additionally, the fact that the former lake bottom was full of mud added pressure and sped up the creek, increasing the erosion and initiating a battle that the dam was doomed to lose. This is the ultimate destiny of all dams.

The mud at the bottom of the former artificial lake is now a very thick and flat-topped layer of soft and unstable topsoil. The present manifestations of Mosquito Creek and Gifford Run have broken themselves up into a delta-like pattern of intertwining channels, creating a weird landscape of mini-canyons and uneven embankments. This has revealed old stumps and other features that were at the bottomland's original level and are many feet below the more recent embankments of silt.

This intensive erosion is still taking place today, and hikers and hunters who are familiar with the area have observed the multiple channels of Mosquito Creek and Gifford Run rerouting themselves and undermining the soft soil above. For example, on the Quehanna Trail you will walk past a hunting camp and then its former driveway. (See the 24.29 mi point in the trail description.) This lane once came in all the way from Caledonia Pike to the south. A little off-trail exploration will reveal that this driveway currently disappears under Gifford Run at a spot where there is simply a sheer cliff of soil on the opposite side. How did the driveway continue?

Previously, hunting camp residents could ford the creek here because the water was shallow enough for rugged vehicles. The driveway then made a sharp turn and continued along the edge of the creek for a while, before

One of several channels of Gifford Run in the Corporation Dam area. The ancient stump once belonged to a tree that sat on the creek's original bottomland. The stump was later buried under about eight feet of mud at the bottom of the former artificial lake, represented by the flat land above the eroded wall of silt behind the stump. The present channel has dug a mini-canyon through the silty soil as the creek seeks to return to its original level, revealing the stump once again. During its lifetime, the tree was probably not in the middle of the creek, indicating that the watercourse was altered by the damaged landscape.

turning again and heading up the opposite hillside. Sometime in the summer of 2014, Gifford Run rerouted itself and undermined the soft soil along its banks. This caused a portion of the former lakebed to collapse, burying the segment of the driveway that was previously parallel to the creek. Now the two surviving segments of the driveway are displaced laterally by a section of Gifford Run that is deeper and narrower than before.

THE QUEHANNA TRAIL AND ITS (LACK OF) FOOTBRIDGES

Back on the Quehanna Trail, this legacy of environmental destruction has made life much more complicated for hikers and trail builders. Efforts to get the trail across Mosquito Creek have resulted in several

The hunting camp driveway, entering from lower left, ends abruptly at a channel of Gifford Run with an eroded wall of silt on the other side. The flat ground above the bank is the former lakebed. Prior to 2014, the stream was closer to the front of this view, but it rerouted itself and caused a small landslide. The driveway formerly made a sharp left turn somewhere in the middle of this view.

collapsed footbridges. The loose soil of the former lakebed complicates the placement of reliable bridges because there are few places to solidly anchor the support piers, while the creek flows more strongly than it would if it was in a more natural landscape.

In the early years of the QT in the 1970s, there was a flimsy cable bridge across Mosquito Creek. A more solid footbridge was eventually built but it was wiped out by a hurricane in 2004. For the next few years, hikers crossed the creek by shimmying across a nearby fallen tree, which itself was later dislodged by rampaging waters and sent away downstream. An expensive fiberglass bridge was constructed in 2007, and it only stood

This photo reveals a prominent section of the former lakebed, in the form of a long berm of soil that is flat on top and about eight feet higher than its surroundings, with an exposed face that has been worn down by a channel of Gifford Run. The area between that stream and the main channel of Mosquito Creek (foreground) is visibly lower. For the past 150 years, periodic floods have eroded the landscape down toward the bottomland's original elevation, but that process is not yet complete.

for four years until its support piers were undermined by a flood in 2011 and the still-intact bridge fell into the creek. The bridge, which was built to last, was hauled up onto the bank for possible reuse but that plan was later abandoned.

That was the state of affairs when the first edition of this book was published in 2015. At that time, DCNR had hatched plans to build another bridge at a more solid spot several hundred yards upstream, but that never happened for various economic and logistical reasons. After several years of a purely wet crossing of the creek for hikers, history repeated itself as someone designated another fallen tree across which to shimmy over the creek. I was surprised to encounter this preposterously unsafe new "route" of the Quehanna Trail in 2020 during a day hike, and when I returned to research this new edition in 2025, I was less surprised to find that this tree had also been swept aside by yet another flood.

At the time of writing in late 2025, the QT's crossing of Mosquito Creek is again a wet crossing, and a potentially dangerous one during high water periods. Also at the time of writing, the 2015 plan for a new bridge a few hundred yards upstream remains a topic of discussion within DCNR, but there has been little progress due to budgetary shortfalls and logistical concerns about transporting significant construction materials to this remote location, which in turn is a considerable distance from the nearest reliable haul road.

Note that any new bridge will require some rerouting of the Quehanna Trail so it can reach whatever solid location has been selected. If this happens the trail is likely to become approximately one-third to one-half of a mile longer in the Mosquito Creek area.

Until a new footbridge is constructed over Mosquito Creek, thru-hiking the Quehanna Trail in this area is not recommended for the typical hiker unless you are prepared to get wet. During low water periods it is reasonably likely that you will find a narrow point in the creek across which to wade, but some exploration up and down the banks to find a favorable spot will be necessary. Regardless, even during low water you face at least a knee-deep wet crossing.

Do not (repeat: DO NOT) attempt this during high water, because the creek's current is very strong and treacherous. Whenever it is in a bad mood, this creek has eroded away an enormous dam, dug canyons into the landscape, and knocked aside several footbridges and large trees. Imagine what it could do to you!

Day hikers on the QT could consider doing the segments on each side of Mosquito Creek as lengthy out-and-back day hikes starting at Lost Run Road to the west and Quehanna Highway to the east. In both cases, turn around at the former bridge crossing and head back to your car.

During high water periods, thru-hikers could consider an extensive detour. From the QT crossing of Lost Run Road, head north then east on that road for about 3 miles to a parking lot near the junction with Reactor Road. Watch for the beginning of Riddle Road—an old lane now used by mountain bikers and horseback riders—which leads about 1.3 miles east to Quehanna Highway near the intersection with Wykoff Run Road. Here, turn southeast on Quehanna Highway and walk about 3.8 miles to the QT crossing near Piper. This detour is actually shorter than the segment of the QT that will be sacrificed. However, you will be skipping 10 miles of the trail, so the detour is not particularly gratifying for the patient hiker who could consider waiting until conditions change.

APPENDIX B:
PIPER AND QUEHANNA WILD AREA

For about 34 miles, from Deserter Run on its southern segment to near Mud Lick Run Road on its northern segment, the Quehanna Trail passes through Quehanna Wild Area. Most of the East Cross Connector Trail, the southern half of the Old Sinnemahoning Trail, and many skiing and equestrian trails are also in the Wild Area. This is the largest such designated area in all of Pennsylvania, and it receives certain types of natural protection. The Wild Area also hosts two small districts with additional protection: Marion Brooks Natural Area and Wykoff Run Natural Area.

According to DCNR rules, a Wild Area is protected to preserve its "wild character" with no new permanent developments allowed. Motorized activities like snowmobiling, vehicular camping, and off-road vehicle use are restricted to approved but limited locations. Nature will be allowed to take its course in the future, with flora and fauna ruling the landscape. These conservation regulations are tougher than those for standard state forest districts.

You will find that Quehanna Wild Area really stretches the meaning of the term "wild" because it is traversed by two long-distance paved roads (Quehanna Highway and Wykoff Run Road) and dozens of dirt roads. There are also a lot of wide pipeline and powerline swaths, and one large dam and artificial lake at Beaver Run Wildlife Viewing Area. DCNR rules even allow limited logging for the supposed purposes of "forest health and wildlife habitat improvements."

The two small Natural Areas receive better protection, and according to DCNR they are "left to the forces of nature, free from human intervention." This is obvious at Marion Brooks Natural Area, where not even hiking trails are allowed. That spot is named after a notable local conservationist and protects what is believed to be the largest stand of white birch trees in the eastern United States. On the other hand, Wykoff Run Natural Area contains former radioactive waste facilities and an old dirt road that is now being used as a ski trail. On the good side, no new development is permitted.

It should be noted that areas that have never experienced human influence are rare in the civilized world and even more so in Pennsylvania, which over the centuries has been drilled, mined, stripped, burned, and clearcut from border to shining border. But efforts are being made to allow previously degraded areas to return to something resembling their original forested state, notwithstanding the legacy of past damage and current management practices. This is indeed the case for Quehanna Wild Area.

HISTORY OF QUEHANNA WILD AREA

The region traversed by the Quehanna Trail is among the most remote in all of Pennsylvania. As late as the 1950s there were no paved roads between Sinnemahoning Creek and the West Branch Susquehanna River, and human habitation was confined to weekend sojourns at hunting camps. To this day there are still no permanent residents in the high plateau area, which is bookended by the tiny village of Medix Run and the slightly larger town of Karthaus.

After World War II, the state made efforts to bring enterprise to this largely inaccessible area, with decidedly mixed results. In the 1950s the Curtiss-Wright corporation, which specialized in military aircraft, sought a secluded area to experiment with top-secret designs for new types of nuclear-powered jet engines. A lucrative contract from the U.S. Department of Defense was secured for experimental research. The company also conducted other nuclear research to develop new peacetime consumer products.

The Quehanna region, then managed as a state forest, was selected for this classified endeavor. Curtiss-Wright purchased a roughly circular area (actually a 16-sided polygon) of about 80 square miles, and the state evicted the hunting camps and literally fenced off the area to all unauthorized outsiders. The area's first paved road, the desolate 23 mile-long Quehanna Highway, was built in 1955 as Curtiss-Wright constructed several industrial facilities.

Most of the buildings were constructed in what is now known as the town of Piper on Quehanna Highway. There was a nuclear reactor a few miles to the northwest just off Lost Run Road, which had been paved and renamed Reactor Road at the time. With the permission of Pennsylvania officials, workers transported radioactive waste downhill from this facility and dumped it in Meeker Run, in an area now traversed by the East Cross Connector Trail.

Some additional facilities for processing experimental substances like beryllium oxide, strontium-90, and cobalt-60, and managing the resulting carcinogenic waste, were built near the present intersection of Quehanna Highway and Wykoff Run Road. The deteriorating paved driveways to these facilities can still be found easily. Curtiss-Wright also made use of an airfield further to the north off Hoover Road, which had been built for airmail deliveries by the Civilian Conservation Corps back in the 1930s.

The region's loggers and miners were hardly qualified for top-secret experimental defense work, so Curtiss-Wright imported skilled technicians and housed them in the planned community of Pine Glen, about ten miles to the southeast on PA 879. Pine Glen is something of a curiosity itself. The now sleepy small town contains several peculiar plus-shaped, multiplexed houses that are oriented perfectly to the four cardinal directions and are shared among multiple families.

The Curtiss-Wright venture did not go well. The company began to abandon parts of the Quehanna operation as soon as 1960 and nuclear-powered aircraft never became a reality. The Department of Defense had lost interest in the technology as well. Pennsylvania re-acquired most of the Curtiss-Wright lands and first established Quehanna Wild Area in 1965, even though the area still contained manufacturing and nuclear facilities.

The Piper Aircraft company, a manufacturer of traditional airplane parts, moved into some of the Curtiss-Wright factory buildings in 1968 and gave its name to the complex. Another aeronautics company, Martin Marietta, performed advanced nuclear research at some of the Curtiss-Wright facilities for a time. Some smaller companies also made use of the nuclear facilities to manufacture experimental products that required irradiation. Piper Aircraft held on until 1984, and nuclear-oriented manufacturing by some smaller companies continued until 2002. Several former factory buildings were demolished in the following years, leaving vast concrete lots behind. As of 2025, the last factory standing is occupied by a company called Nydree that makes custom hardwood flooring.

Today the remote "town" of Piper does not have any actual residents or consumer businesses. The Quehanna Trail passes about half a mile to the north, and I have seen descriptions of the trail in books and magazines telling hikers that "services" can be found in Piper. This is false. There are no stores or restaurants, or even homeowners to invite you in for a glass of lemonade. Piper contains a PennDOT (Pennsylvania Department of Transportation) heavy equipment garage; in an extreme emergency you might find some employees there to offer assistance.

Another longtime occupant of the complex has been a minimum-security prison called Quehanna Boot Camp, though at the time of writing this facility is not long for this world. In 2025, the Pennsylvania Department of Corrections announced a plan to close Quehanna Boot Camp as a cost-cutting measure because of declining prison populations across the state prison system. As this book goes to press, the prison is scheduled to close by mid-2026 and its many buildings will revert to DCNR ownership for some undecided future use.

Quehanna Boot Camp is (was) an unconventional incarceration facility for nonviolent offenders serving short sentences, and others whom a judge deemed to be deserving of an alternative to hard time in prison. The convicts are put through a six-month program that is indeed based on the military boot camp experience, with tough mental discipline and physical fitness. The facility also handles offenders with substance abuse problems, who are put through a 24-month program of counseling, treatment, and education. The guards are only lightly armed. Motorists driving up Quehanna Highway are likely to see inmates exercising outdoors while overseen by laidback guards. Inmates are also involved in community work endeavors, including state forest maintenance and trail building. Over the facility's history, almost all inmates completed their programs successfully and were returned to society on probation, and despite the wide-open grounds and relaxed supervision, there were only a few attempted escapes.

CURRENT AND FUTURE CONSERVATION

Much like Corporation Dam on Mosquito Creek (see Appendix A), short-lived industrial ventures in the Piper area have resulted in decades of environmental degradation and cleanup. There are an estimated 180 contaminated sites in what is now Quehanna Wild Area.

Some toxic waste was simply buried in the woods when Curtiss-Wright abandoned its facilities. The remains of the concrete bunkers that processed carcinogenic waste near the intersection of Quehanna Highway and Wykoff Run Road are still visible to the trained eye along the Old Hoover Trail in Wykoff Run Natural Area. The buildings were buried in soil and now resemble tiny hills jutting abruptly above a flat area, with a covering of thin trees that do not look particularly healthy. Until about 2003, that area was posted with signs warning hikers and hunters of possible toxic contamination.

The nuclear reactor near Lost Run Road had been sealed off and was finally demolished in 2008. There was still so much lingering radioactivity that robots were required for the task, and access to the site is still restricted. At various other sites, contaminated soil was dug up and replaced while some small buildings were buried. The cleanup cost for all these toxic facilities has been over $30 million—an amount distressingly similar to what Curtiss-Wright originally paid for the land back in 1955.

The state allows hunting and primitive camping in Quehanna Wild Area, concluding that (usually) there is minimal danger from radioactive or toxic contamination. However, there have been some reports of buried toxic material being dug up by bears. There are also no special regulations for fishing, so the conclusion has been reached that the area's streams are reasonably safe. There are a few posted areas that are still off limits, and all outdoorspersons should take those boundaries seriously. But otherwise, hikers, hunters, fishermen, birdwatchers, skiers, and everyone else are welcome to enjoy Quehanna Wild Area. There will be very few if any ill effects, and we are lucky to have such a large area in which to experience nature.

APPENDIX C:
MEDIX RUN AND THE BEAR RUN TRAIL

Through most of its history, the northwestern section of the Quehanna Trail had an Achilles heel at the crossing of the usually placid but sometimes vicious Medix Run. In an area now traversed by the Bear Run Trail, the original route of the QT reached this creek about 1.3 miles southwest of Quehanna Highway at Haystack Mountain, crossed on a bridge, and proceeded west toward Parker Dam State Park.

For most of the year, the rather sizeable creek is much too wide to hop across on rocks, and a pattern of slow-moving wide spots interrupted by much faster and narrower defiles adds to the challenge of building footbridges.

When the Quehanna Trail reached the area in 1977, it crossed Medix Run on a 135-foot-long footbridge at a spot just downstream from what is now a reservable car campsite on Medix Grade Road. This bridge survived until 1991 when it had to be removed for safety purposes because the wood was rotting away. The design of that bridge should have been retained because then the bad luck really began.

For about the next three years, QT hikers had to endure a wet crossing of the creek. A much shorter bridge, just 48 feet long over a narrower part of the creek, was not completed until late 1994. Just 14 months later in early 1996, a flash flood with the added power of ice washed away one of the support piers and twisted the whole bridge like a pretzel. The superstructure of the bridge actually survived the mishap, and hikers could still use it after some minor repairs. The creek continued to dig away at the support apparatus, so reinforcements and diversion dams were added in 2001 and 2011. [Seeley, 30]

All was well until early 2014, when another flash flood ripped this much-coddled bridge completely off its support piers and smashed it like a shipwreck on the creekside. As in a previous mishap, it remained

The state of affairs after a major reroute in the
Quehanna Trail network in 2016.

intact but was contorted into a bizarre shape, in addition to no longer even crossing the creek. This time the bridge was not rehabilitated, and the hiker was forced to endure a wet crossing of Medix Run yet again.

In 2016, DCNR gave up on this unlucky bridge location. Since the Quehanna Trail is designated as an official state forest hiking trail, more hikers are expected to explore it as compared to less-promoted trails elsewhere. Due to liability issues caused by all these potential visitors, the decision was made to reroute the QT around Medix Run altogether. Thus, the last wrecked bridge was never replaced.

Southwest of Quehanna Highway at Haystack Mountain, the QT follows a pipeline swath above and parallel to Medix Grade Road. Prior to 2016 it turned west off the swath and headed toward the creek. In that year, the QT was rerouted to remain on the pipeline, southbound, for about another mile. The new route emerges on Medix Grade Road and then turns west on Little Medix Road to a junction with the West Cross Connector Trail. The new version of the QT then appropriates the former route of the West Cross Connector Trail and heads west to Saunders Road where it finally rejoins its original route.

This extensive rerouting made the West Cross Connector Trail more than three miles shorter than it was before 2016, while the abandoned segment of the QT is more than five miles long. This is one of the major factors that caused significantly different trail measurements for both the QT and QTWCC in this book as compared to its first edition in 2015.

The demoted segment of the QT was then rechristened as the Bear Run Trail, which as an apparently less-visited spur trail is permitted to have the now bridgeless crossing of Medix Run, where the intrepid hiker will get wet for most of the year. There are two silver linings to this story: the Quehanna Trail no longer has a wet crossing of the creek, while the Bear Run Trail does have a wet crossing but features the pleasant scenery and solitude of the original QT that dedicated hikers can still fully enjoy.

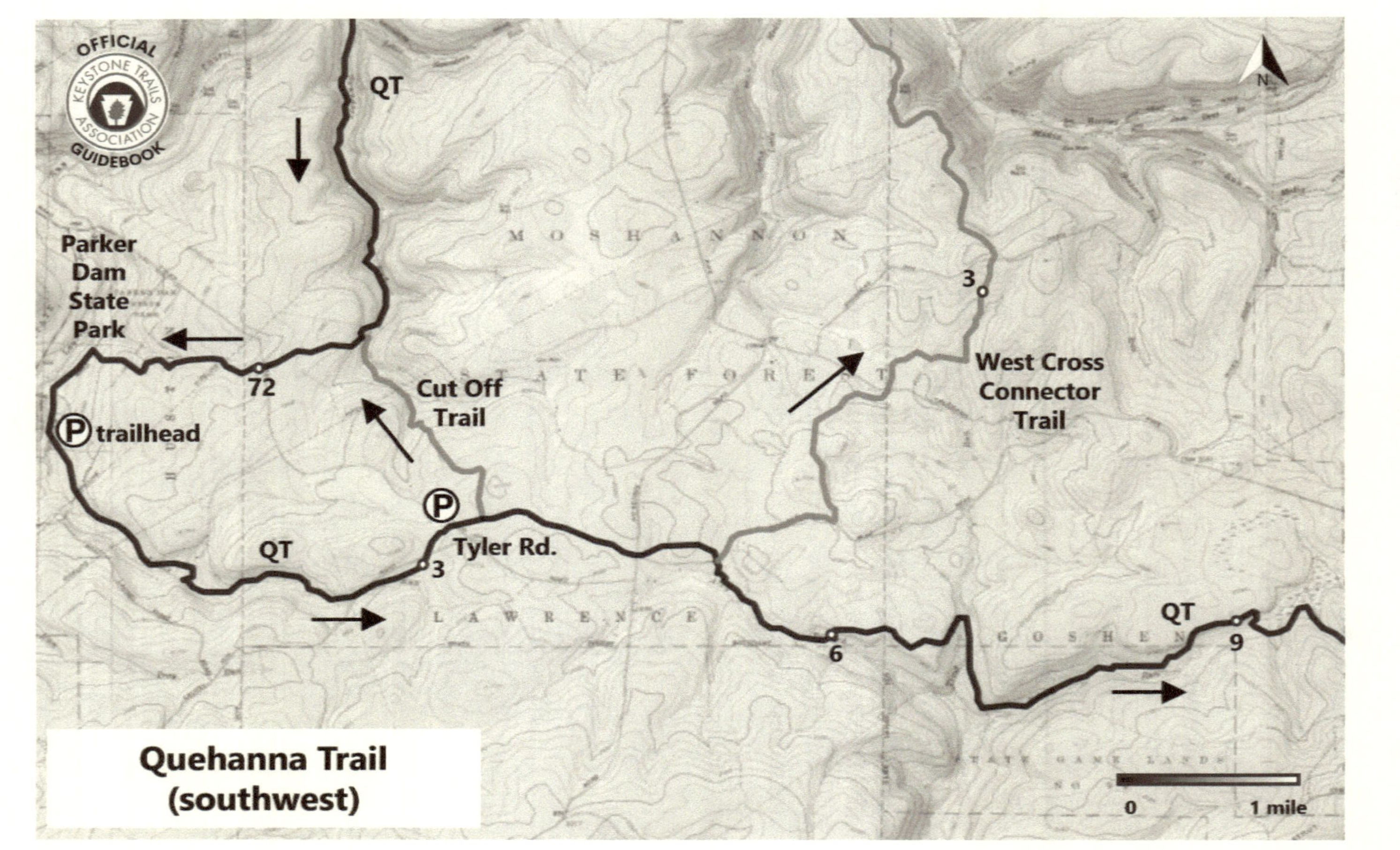

OFFICIAL
KEYSTONE TRAILS ASSOCIATION
GUIDEBOOK
N
QT
Parker
Dam
State
Park
72
P trailhead
QT
3
P
Tyler Rd.
3
Cut Off
Trail
West Cross
Connector
Trail
MOSHANNON
STATE FOREST
LAWRENCE
GOSHEN
STATE GAME LANDS
6
QT
9
Quehanna Trail
(southwest)
0   1 mile

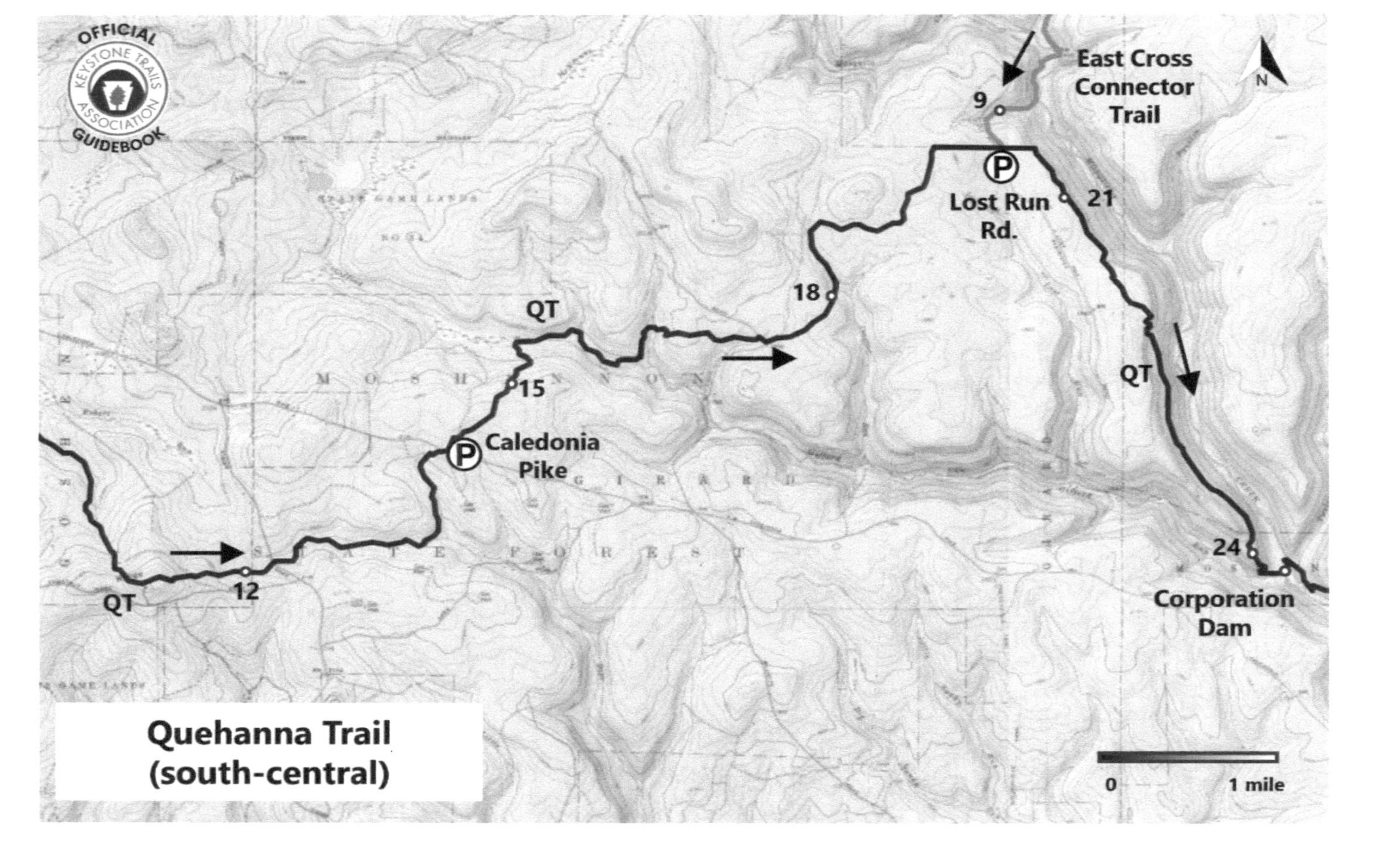

OFFICIAL KEYSTONE TRAILS ASSOCIATION GUIDEBOOK
N
East Cross Connector Trail
9
Lost Run Rd.
21
18
QT
15
QT
Caledonia Pike
12
QT
24
Corporation Dam
Quehanna Trail (south-central)
0   1 mile

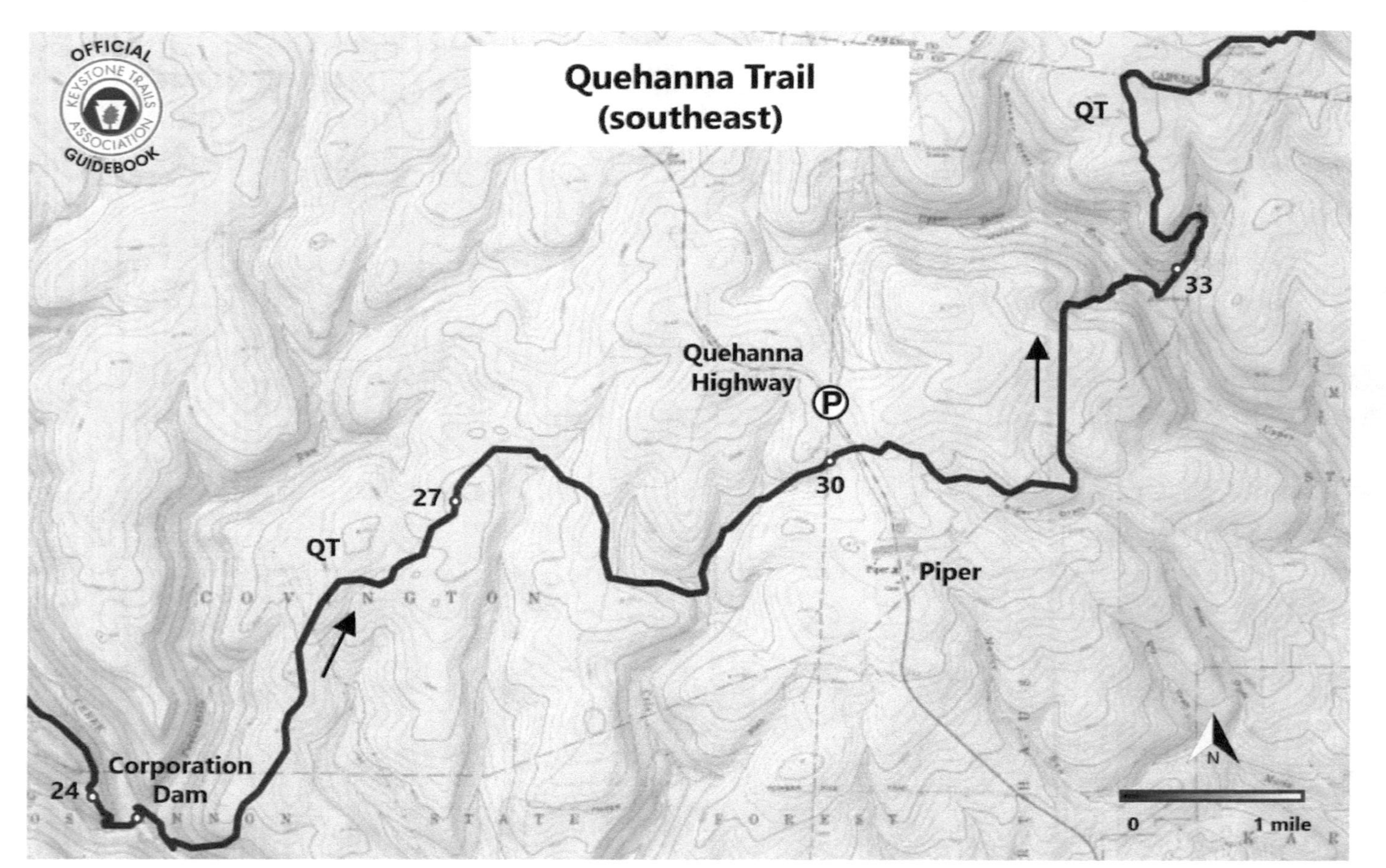

OFFICIAL
KEYSTONE TRAILS ASSOCIATION
GUIDEBOOK
Quehanna Trail
(southeast)
QT
33
Quehanna
Highway
P
30
Piper
27
QT
Corporation
Dam
24
N
0
1 mile

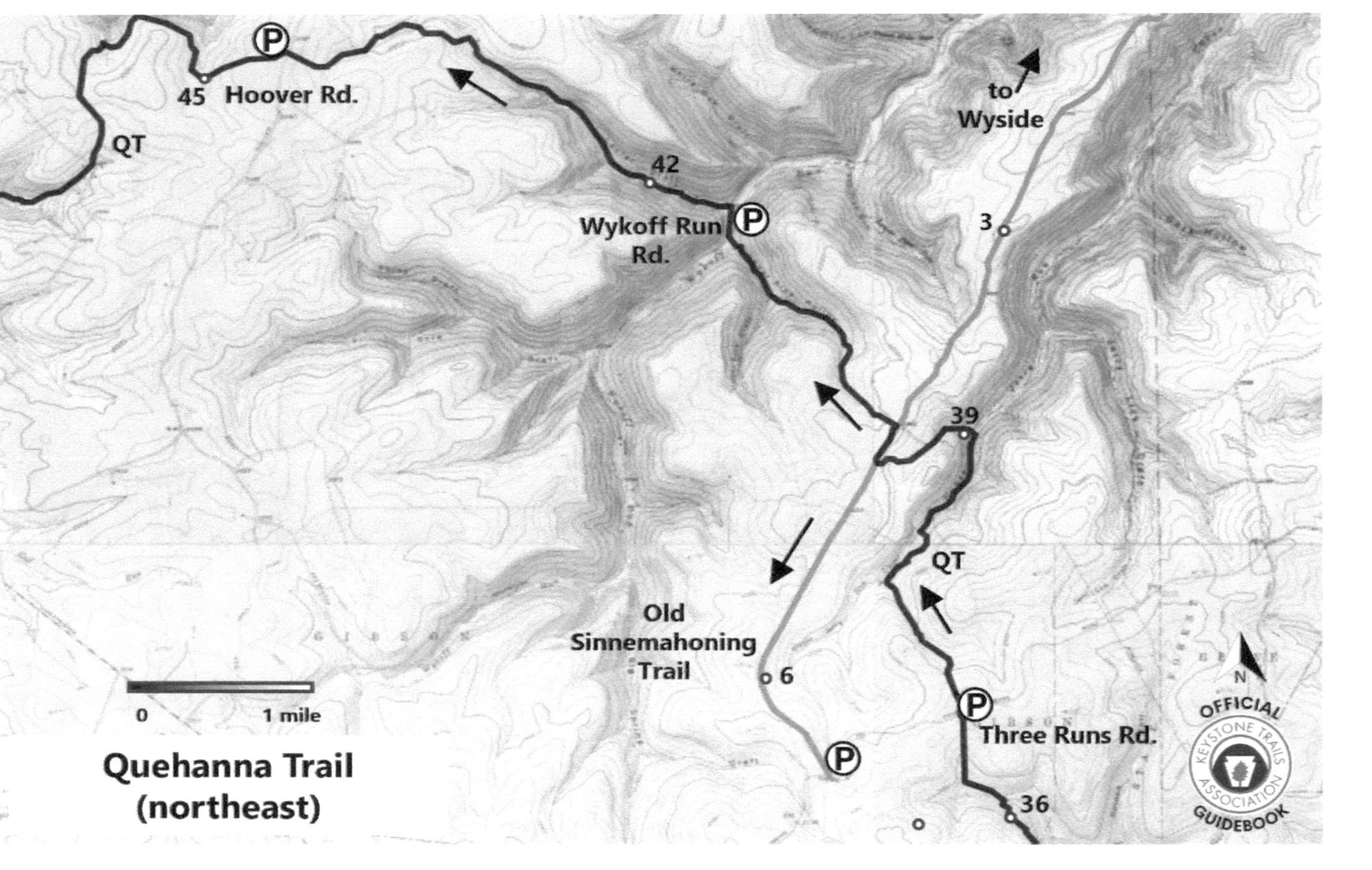

Quehanna Trail (northeast)

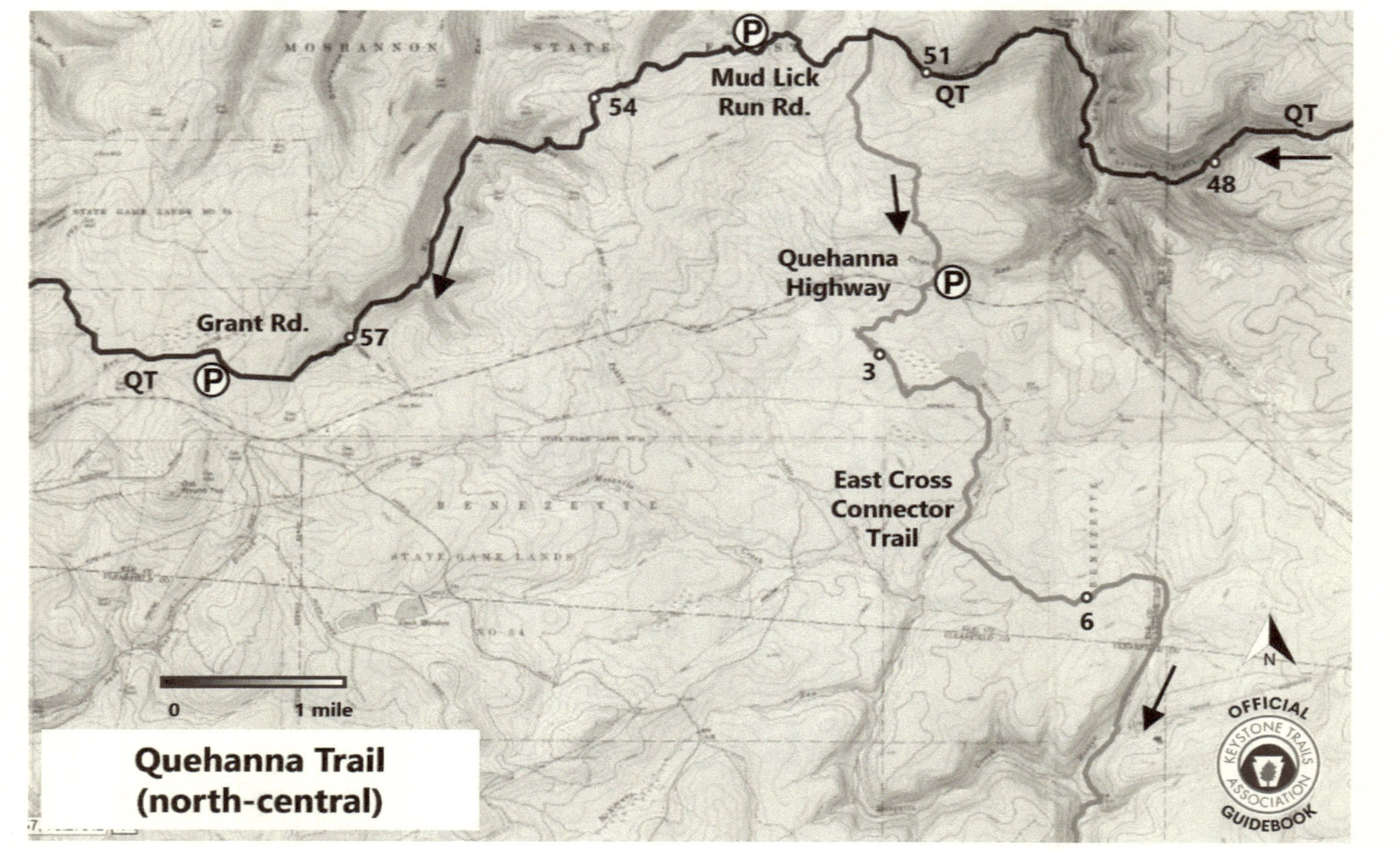

MOSHANNON STATE
Mud Lick Run Rd.
54
51
QT
QT
48
Quehanna Highway
3
East Cross Connector Trail
Grant Rd.
57
QT
BENEZETTE
STATE GAME LANDS
6
N
0   1 mile
Quehanna Trail (north-central)
OFFICIAL
KEYSTONE TRAILS ASSOCIATION
GUIDEBOOK

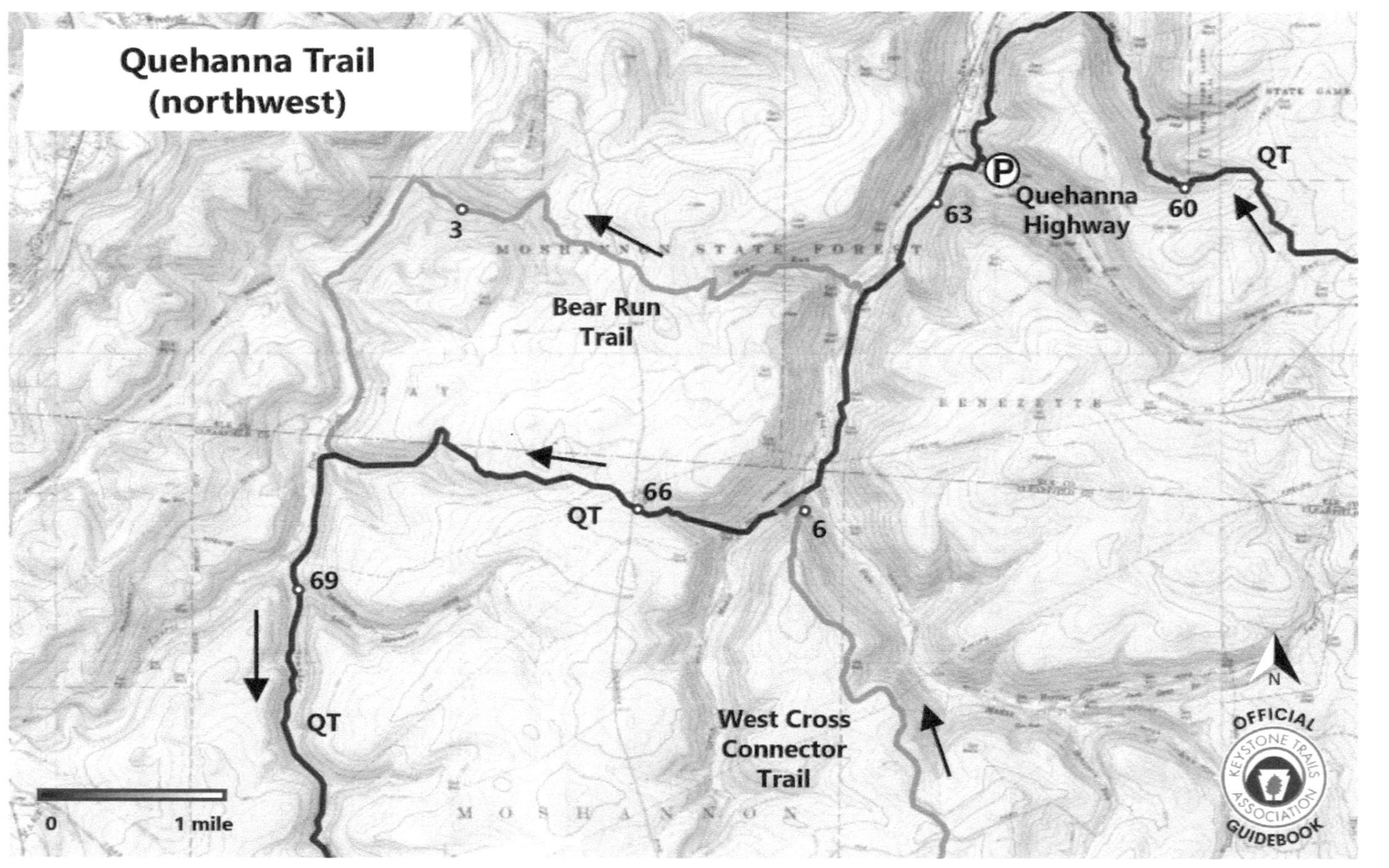

Quehanna Trail
(northwest)
QT
60
63
Quehanna
Highway
Bear Run
Trail
3
66
QT
6
69
QT
West Cross
Connector
Trail
N
0
1 mile
OFFICIAL
GUIDEBOOK
KEYSTONE TRAILS ASSOCIATION

For a larger online map of the Quehanna Trail network,
visit Keystone Trails Association at:

www.kta-hike.org/maps

or scan here:

These maps illustrate GPS data collected by the author. The online map is courtesy of CalTopo. The printed map on the previous two pages was created with GPS Visualizer, founded and operated by Adam Schneider, with USGS (United States Geologic Survey) maps as the backgrounds. All maps and data are verified for accuracy by the author and Keystone Trails Association.

ABOUT THE AUTHOR

Ben Cramer has hiked more than 6,000 miles on Pennsylvania's hiking trails and has completed many of the state's long-distance backpacking trails multiple times. He is a longtime member of Keystone Trails Association, and was a member of its board of directors from 2018 to 2023. He is also a member of several Pennsylvania conservation groups and hiking clubs, and was formerly an executive committee member for Sierra Club at both the local and state levels.

Cramer is the author of seven guidebooks for Pennsylvania backpacking trails, including one previous edition for the Quehanna Trail. With one exception, none of those long-distance trails had dedicated guidebooks previously. Cramer was also the editor of *Pennsylvania Hiking Trails* (13th edition, 2008). For several years he wrote regularly on outdoor adventure and environmental issues for *The Centre Daily Times* and for a variety of Pennsylvania volunteer publications.

Under his professional name Benjamin W. Cramer, he is the author of the book *Freedom of Environmental Information* (2011). He is a longtime resident of State College, PA and teaches for the Donald P. Bellisario College of Communications at Penn State University, where one of his research specialties is the environmental impacts of modern telecommunications services.